MW00666965

Without Rule of Law

Advanced Skills to Help You Survive

By Joe Nobody

Published by Prepper Press

Publishing to Help You Prepare

See Joe Nobody's other books by visiting

www.PrepperPress.com or

www.HoldingYourGround.com

Copyright 2012

Kemah Bay Marketing LTD.

All rights reserved

WARNING

Some of the exercises, ideas, maneuvers and devices included in this book are dangerous and could cause injury or death.

You should not attempt any of these activities without proper training, safety measures and safety equipment being applied and/or implemented.

Some of the exercises in this work are physically demanding and could result in injury or death. You should not attempt any exercise without being certain of your capability to do so without negative results.

You agree to hold harmless the publisher, author and all associated with **WITHOUT RULE OF LAW**, regardless of circumstance or event.

By proceeding, you are agreeing to accept full responsibility for your own actions and any results of those actions. No liability can be assumed or placed with the publisher, author or anyone associated with **WITHOUT RULE OF LAW**.

Contents

WITHOUT RULE OF LAW

Advanced Skills to Help You Survive

Prologue

I didn't want to write this book. It goes against my grain. I am a positive, optimistic person, and the subject matter of this work is dark and foreboding.

It speaks of a time when my meticulous preparations fail, and I have to resort to the very behavior that I have campaigned to eradicate. It advocates and teaches skills and actions that I despise in others. Yet, the very creed of self-reliance is preparing---for whatever may happen. Are we so confident that the proverbial Shit will Hit The Fan (SHTF) only one time? Where is it written that society will immediately bounce back, returning civilization quickly to its pre-SHTF state? Is there no such thing as The End Of The World As We Know It (TEOTWAWKI) II? What happens when my preparations are not enough?

Our forefathers possessed skills that we respect, in which they lived valuable lives without the advantages of electricity and other modern conveniences. Despite all of their self-reliance, skills, and knowledge, disaster still struck. Drought, Indian raids, war, and even weather that destroyed crops endangered their lives. They often struggled to survive, despite all of their preparations. In a post-SHTF society, there will likely be no resources for an already starving population if a natural disaster strikes.

If this is depressing to think about, do what we preppers always do when faced with a plausible doomsday scenario – pull up your big boy pants and settle on a plan where we persevere - no matter what. Let's plan on pulling out all the stops to insure survival.

Let me share with you a bit about what I mean. My family and I have enough provisions to survive about six months at our bug out location with what we have on hand. Our plan is to begin harvesting some crops within 3-6 months of our relocation there, depending on the growing season. Here in Texas, our climate allows a good amount of latitude where our growing season is concerned. But what if a second disaster somehow prevented our harvest? As I write this text, Texas is in a record-breaking drought. Luckily, my Bug Out Location (BOL) is not as dry as much of the surrounding area and probably is fertile enough to sustain some growth. However, most of the state is plagued with stressed, dry, and even dead trees, affecting everything from 40-foot pines to century old oaks. Suppose my BOL neighbor accidentally started a fire while smoking meat, and the woods were suddenly ablaze. Is it hard to imagine a time when societal resources do not provide for social amenities like local fire departments? If our nation is struggling to establish law and order, how much more can it handle? What will happen when our resources are depleted? How will we survive then?

Without Rule of Law assumes that such a time arrives when anarchy is pervasive, and the remnants of humanity are struggling to re-establish civilization. Governmental resources are thin or nonexistent. Do you have a plan for this contingency? What additional skills or means would you need on hand to prepare for this?

Certainly, those who survive in such a situation will do so largely due to advanced survival know-how. Now the idea of honing some of these skills might make you a little uncomfortable while you lounge in your climate-controlled home, nibbling on Chinese takeout and watching HBO. But I challenge you to move out of your comfort zone and consider just what may be at stake. These additional skills may save your life or the life of someone you love. But what kind of skills are we talking about anyway? Well, let me give you an example.

I will make you a bet. I will wager that I can walk from the north side of any American city to the south side carrying a full combat load, including M4 rifle, 200 rounds of ammo, body armor and load vest. I will perform this task in broad daylight without the police or anyone else taking notice.

I will make another wager after I collect on the first. You can pick any factory, strip mall or other public facility and I will spend the entire day on the property, without anyone seeing me. I will walk to and from the target carrying all of my survival gear, which would most likely cause the local SWAT team to be dispatched if I were discovered.

Want to go for double or nothing? You can pick any area at least 800 meters square. I will hide in that area. You and a friend have four hours to find me. I don't care if it is woods, open field, urban or suburban territory, you won't find me.

How about playing the prison break game? Give me a 15-minute head start and see if you and some friends can catch me. Bring your ATM card, friend – you are going to need it.

Am I a super spy? A Special Forces operator? A military sniper? No, I am just like you ... a Joe Nobody. My only advantage is that I understand a few basic tenants of human behavior, observation, and camouflage. I require less than $100 worth of equipment (not counting weapon and ammo) to execute these tasks.

After reading this book, you will be able to do all of the above and more. Perhaps these skills may save your life one day.

INTRODUCTION

The purpose of this book is to provide an instructional reference regarding four advanced skill sets to be used while living in a long-term SHTF or TEOTWAWKI environment.

Specifically, it addresses how to equip, train, and execute the following:

Hide

Evade

Infiltrate

Scavenge

It was difficult to research some of these tactical actions. Where do you go for expertise? Militaries commonly teach survival courses that cover some of these topics, but they are intended to get a soldier back into friendly hands.

We preppers, in a post-SHTF world, probably won't have any friendly forces to rescue us.

Snipers utilize many of the skills covered in this book, and a wealth of knowledge was obtained from that source. With all due respect to these brave and highly skilled soldiers, modern snipers operate in teams with an array of high tech equipment unavailable to the typical prepper.

We will probably be operating alone.

The capabilities of the U.S. Special Forces are probably the closest match to what it will take to survive without the rule of law. One of their primary mission profiles is to integrate with indigenous populations and convert them into organized fighting forces. These special operators are without support for extended periods of time, often in enemy territory. They are known for their creativity and adaptability. They are also quietly known as world-class scavengers. With that being said, we can take advantage of the skills and knowledge of these men and adapt them to a non-military situation.

Again, we preppers will want to avoid the indigenous people and remain totally self-reliant.

A salute of respect goes to the British Commandos of WWII. These brave men wrote much of the manual when it comes to non-direct military actions. I found many useful tactics from the study of their operations. Today, their exploits may seem insipid compared to modern capabilities. Consider though that in the 1940's, **no one** had done anything like what they attempted. They received a very hard education, and so many of them paid the tuition with their blood.

A highly trained and experienced military operator could accomplish most of the skills contained herein without much difficulty. We preppers, on the other hand, are probably not in peak physical condition and are definitely not high speed, low drag individuals. We have children, jobs and commitments that prohibit us from rigorous training regiments and constantly improving our skills. From this perspective, I attempted to dull the edge of the sword – just slightly. If you are in reasonable physical condition and have the right attitude, you can perform all of the activities recommended here. I hope no one ever has to utilize the content of this book. If an event ever does occur, my prayers will be for us all.

Joe Nobody

1. HOW TO USE THIS BOOK

Each of the four skills addressed in this work require some level of preparation, planning, equipment and practice.

Each chapter contains sections describing the following:

> Recommended equipment (specific to the skill)
> Steps to prepare
> Exercises, practice routines or activities
> Example plans (where applicable)

Practically every business, military unit, sports team, or band prepares a plan and then practices or rehearses. Preppers are a little different. We often plan, gather equipment and stockpile supplies, but rarely train on the skills that may be required to survive. This isn't meant as a criticism. It is impossible to predict any given scenario since TEOTWAWKI has never occurred – at least not in recent history. Since we don't know what our lives will be like, training often seems unrealistic or misapplied. No one wants to waste time developing skills that may never be used.

For this reason, the example practice routines and activities provided are designed to be entertaining or perhaps, even fun. Don't confuse the levity of the proposed exercises with the seriousness of the topic. **Get off of the couch, and go do some of the activities.** You will be surprised at what you learn, and you may enjoy the day.

EXERCISE

This symbol (above) indicates an exercise that can be performed to improve your capabilities.

As you progress through the chapters, the example plans provided build upon the previous section's examples. The skills become progressively more complex and thus require a more detailed plan. It is important to actually take the time to write out your plan as you go through the book. The combination of the exercises and creating a plan will point out problems that are easily solved now rather than after a collapse.

This book recommends a systematic, layered planning approach, beginning with four simple steps:

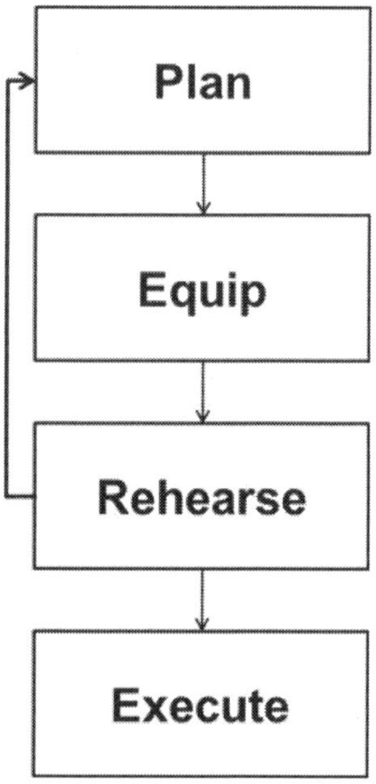

As the skills become more involved, the operational plan will include multiple tactical phases combined into a single unit. An example of a phase would be setting up bivouac, or a position for the night. This activity involves its own timeline, equipment, rehearsal, and execution. Ask yourself the following questions:

Do you know how long it takes to set up for the night?

Do you have an equipment checklist already made for this purpose?

Can you execute this relatively simple task in the dark or with low light?

How long does it take to break down your campsite and prepare to move on?

While setting up camp for the night seems like such a simple act, if it is not properly executed, the failure to get adequate rest for the night can completely foul a more complex scavenging operation. Exceeding the time allocated to break down camp can cause a domino effect on the entire schedule.

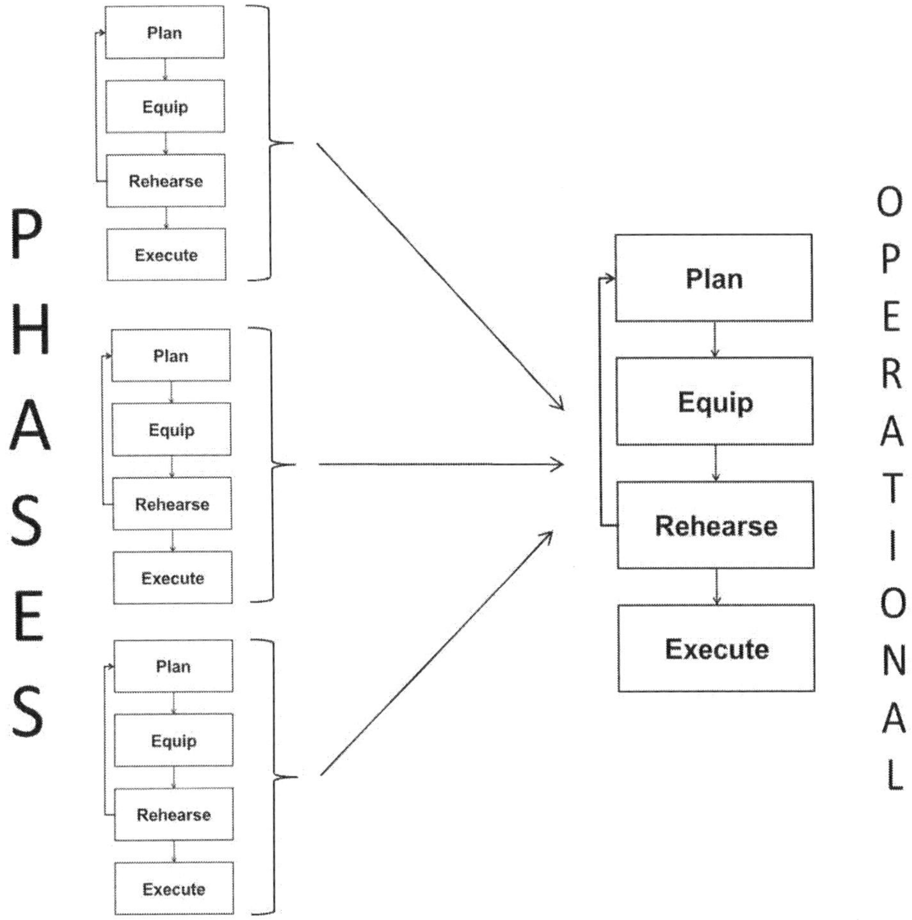

As you progress through the book, the tactical phases will be noted and included in the more complex operational plans.

All of this book's content, activities, and exercises are legal at the author's locale. **Don't assume that they are legal where you live.** The justification of, "But your honor, I read it in a book," won't get you very far in most courtrooms.

Finally, the majority of the content assumes a single person is performing the suggested activities. The book was written this way intentionally as it is the worst-case scenario. Clearly, a small team, or group of people, could be more affective. The addition of communications and a coordinated plan would be all that is required to expand the number of participants. There is a later chapter addressing more of the specifics involved with group operations.

2. THE METHODOLOGY OF PREPARING

I like to include this methodology in all of my books. None of us really know that TEOTWAWKI is going to occur. After years of investing time, energy, and money into preparations, one could easily become discouraged with the preparation process when doing so seems like a waste of time and effort. I address this issue personally by sticking to the process as outlined below.

When it comes to any type of preparation activity, here are some example rules and tests that can applied to this process:

i. **Do No Harm** – Do not implement any plan that will harm:
   - The value of my property
   - The lifestyle of my family
   - My moral character
   - My code of life and behavior
   - My position as a law-abiding citizen and patriot

ii. **Dual Purpose –** Any investment in equipment, time, stress, or training should serve a dual purpose. This is so that over the long-term, frustration, and *buyer's remorse* do not occur.

   Example: Camping gear can be dual purposed for, of all things, CAMPING! This is a recreational activity, something fun and useful. Since I live in Texas, close enough to the coast to have to bug out in case of a hurricane, a likely event, our bug out bag (BOB) is dual purpose.

iii. **People will be the biggest problem.** In this methodology, people are to be avoided. Plans, equipment, and supplies are all derived with an emphasis on AVOIDING PEOPLE.

iv. **You and your family are people, and thus, still the biggest problem.** So much has been written about the mental state of survival that it does not need repeating here. However, anything to be included in the plan should improve the mental state of the group, or at minimum, not degrade it.

v. **When it comes to equipment or skills, consider the military a field testing unit.** Many have noted that military grade equipment is designed to be used by conscripts with little training under high stress conditions. It is also designed to last for long periods of time in the field under harsh environmental conditions. With weapons, such as the AR15, it is difficult to find a larger stockpile of ammo, spare parts, general knowledge, and interchangeable components for any other weapon in the U.S. Some equipment can be significantly less expensive if sourced at Army Surplus stores.

The military is NOT the best at everything, including gear. Consider the example of backpacks. The regular issue military pack is not nearly as comfortable as a custom fit pack from a quality hiking supplier. I look first to the military for tactics and equipment, but always see what the private sector provides as well. Traditional retailers are often able to offer more individualized solutions that military suppliers cannot.

vi. **Everything must work at night.** Half of the time, everyone is going to be in low-light conditions. Want to have some fun? Ask your children to set up a tent at night. Make sure to film a video for YouTube of this exercise. *My family is set up to drive, eat, camp, and operate weapons at night.* One word of warning – operating at night, in a covert way, is EXPENSIVE. This normally involves Night Vision Device (NVD) or Forward-Looking Infrared (FLIR) equipment. If your location enables you to simply use candles without concern for #3 above (people seeing the light), then a large expense can be avoided.

So before adding any piece of equipment, plan, or action, follow the methodology:

1. Will taking this step or creating this item hurt property value? Will it do any harm?

2. Can we get dual usage out of this purchase or exercise? Will it help in day-to-day life or even be useful in a hurricane (or other common event) plan? Is there a way this can be fun?
3. Are other people needed to operate or execute? Will executing this plan help avoid other people or enable more independence?
4. Can the family competently operate the equipment or execute the task? Will doing so make our lives easier or cause additional hardship? Can this eliminate hardship?
5. How does this task or equipment compare to military models? What can we take from their experience?
6. What are our capabilities to use this method or equipment at night?

I hope everyone will perform the same tests or establish similar rules in conjunction with the exercises and recommendations of this book.

3. MODIFIED MASLOW

My preparations involve "the ranch," which is an isolated track of land 150 miles away from my primary, suburban residence. Like many of you, we (my family of four) are bug out preppers. We can have the pickup truck loaded with supplies, ammunition, equipment, and firearms in less than two hours. Our short-term needs are packed in plastic storage bins and fit nicely in the bed of the truck. A quick spin of the gun safe locks, and we are off and running to our BOL (bug out location), where the long-term supplies are stockpiled and ready for our needs. We are confident in the parameters of this plan because we live in hurricane country and have had to bug out a few times in the past. If a few years go by without a storm, we all practice to keep everything fresh.

There are, however, several flaws with our well-rehearsed strategy. Really, for such a simple act as driving 150 miles, there are countless potential issues. For example, the truck could be shot out from under us. Martial law could be declared, and the roads closed before we can relocate. Obstacles don't even have to be anything dramatic or related to TEOTWAWKI at all. The mundane, everyday event of a truck breaking down could complicate the plan.

You can drive yourself nuts trying to prepare for all of this. What is a prepper to do? How do you, within reason, plan for all of the eventualities? If you let your mind run with this long enough, eventually you will be trying to prepare for Godzilla stepping on your garden and ruining the crop. I haven't figured out a way to prepare for every single eventuality. It is beyond me or anyone else I have ever met.

What you can do is develop advanced capabilities that are broad based and generic in nature. Like a multi-tool of personal skills, they may not serve as well as the specific wrench, but can get the job done. Creating this inventory of capabilities is really a simple task. These advanced skills are really nothing more than a few basic skills, combined together with suitable equipment and properly sequenced execution. The confidence and sense of preparedness you will feel is worth the effort. Many people would not give my family much of a chance of traveling 150 miles on foot, through a potentially hostile post-collapse countryside. My wife and I aren't spring chickens anymore and have the same sore backs, aching knees and general aliments associated with latter middle age.

Many people in their prime would not consider putting on very heavily loaded packs and attempting a hike of that duration, especially if society were falling off the edge all around them. Yet, we all feel like we could make it. Some of this sureness is a product of practice and experience. We have hiked high desert mountains and navigated remote trails of over 20 miles or more. We know we can do it, and that is one of the biggest hurdles to any plan.

Given the scenario of our truck breaking down, we could deal with it. It would be uncomfortable and require an extreme effort, but we would overcome without permanently impairing our bug out plan. A key to our confidence is an elementary understanding of our *needs*.

It wouldn't make any difference if the situation involved a bug in urban apartment dweller or a rancher in the great southwest. Anything can happen regardless of how well you prepare. When I was a younger man, the bright lights of the city attracted me like a moth to flame. I lived in several high-rise apartment buildings and experienced the city lifestyle. In those days, still during the cold war, the potential exchange of hydrogen warheads was going to cause TEOTWAWAKI. My plan as a bold, seemingly invincible young man involved mostly living by the gun. It is no coincidence that I had the same exact *needs* with my preparations then as what I do now even though my concept of preparing has changed dramatically.

Many members of my family live in rural, country environments. They inhabit areas that have raw acreage, few people, and abundant natural resources. When we have worked through their preparations, the list and priority of *needs* always come out the same for my suburban family today and as the lists made for the folks who have opted to live in the pastoral settings of my youth.

So what are these needs?

Almost everyone is familiar with Maslow's Hierarchy of Needs. Regardless of your level of acceptance of Maslow, establishing basic skills and then building upon them is a widely accepted method of adult learning. "Walk before you run" and "Learn the basics first" are repeated throughout most teaching processes. In order to execute the skills addressed in this book, there is a specific hierarchy relating to both capabilities and equipment.

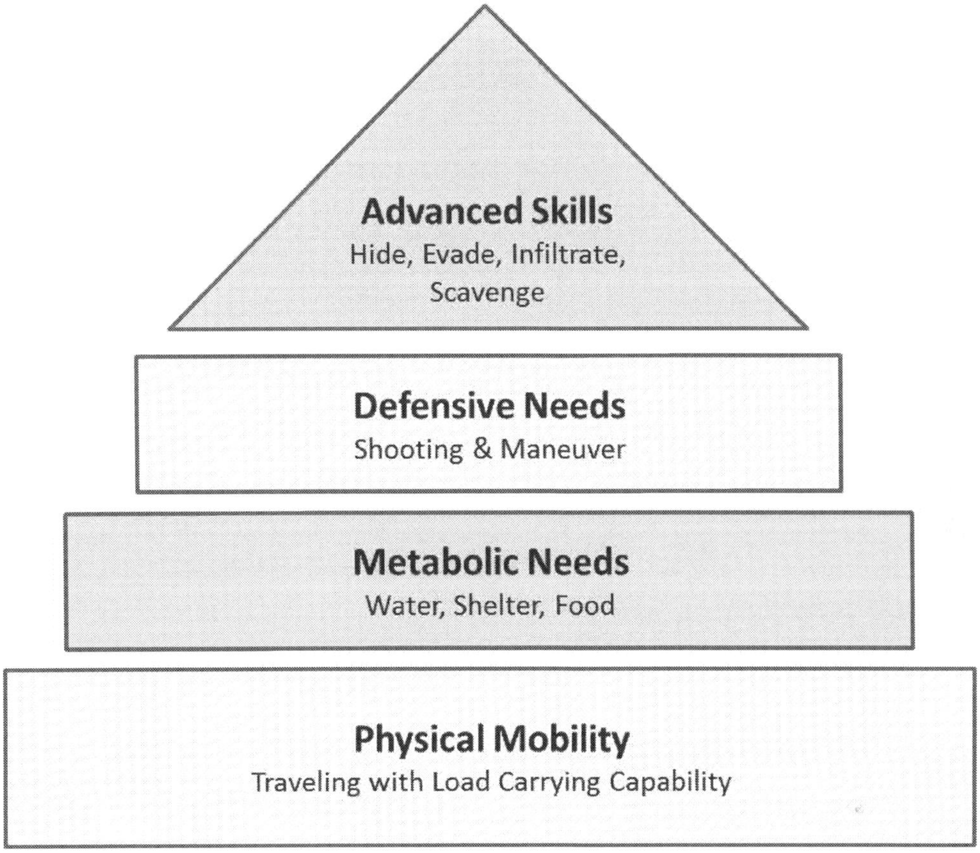

Before the advanced skills at the top of the pyramid can be achieved, it is mandatory to master the building blocks, or foundational elements at the bottom. After all, what good does it do to know everything about breaching if you can't travel to and from the target building?

If my family and I were to attempt the aforementioned bug out and suddenly find ourselves without a truck, we can still be mobile. All of our critical equipment is contained within backpacks. (**Physical Mobility**) These packs include our **Metabolic Needs**. Strapping on a load vest and a rifle will address the **Defensive Needs**. Since we are mobile, metabolically stable (we can eat and drink), and can defend ourselves, then we are ready to execute the advanced skills such as hiding. As we work our way, on foot, toward our BOL, we can hide, evade, and scavenge along the way.

Even if our truck never made it out of the driveway, we can still survive. The fact that we are trained, equipped, and capable of satisfying the four levels of the pyramid above gives everyone confidence. We, however, do not consider ourselves invincible. That would be foolish. Life can throw an unlimited number of challenges our way. Our self-assurance is based on the fact that we have prepared as much as is reasonable. We have done what we can. We have addressed our needs.

In summary, our modified hierarchy of needs translates into the following capabilities:

(1) Travel long distances on foot while carrying all of your critical equipment.

(2) The environment is assumed to be reasonably dangerous; therefore, the ability to utilize defensive equipment, such as a rifle, is vital.

(3) Having some survival equipment on your person at all times is important. Even if an outing of limited duration is planned, you never know when some rogue or hostile group is going to get between you and your domain. You might be pursued or even lost while scavenging.

(4) The ability to Bivouac (camp) overnight is assumed. This coincides with carrying survival equipment at all times.

This list should be similar to everyone's normal survival needs. Given that we want to stay within the rules of our methodology, the equipment required to execute these actions can also be used for hunting, hiking, climbing, or camping. While some people take these recreational activities seriously and purchase top quality equipment, others do not. If you are a casual camper, then please consider that the skills listed above become critical in a survival situation. Failure becomes life or death, not simply a wasted weekend hiking trip or miserable camping experience.

While all of the tactical abilities described in this book require some specialized equipment, there are certain foundational items you will need in order to execute **any** of the techniques described. If a unique piece of gear is required for a specific skill, it will be covered at the beginning of that chapter.

The appendices at the back of this book contain reference material on various equipment options and carry systems. If you are a beginning Prepper or have never served, you may want to read the book ***The TEOWTAWKI Tuxedo: Formal Survival Attire***, which addresses the integration of personal survival and defensive equipment with load bearing systems.

The relationship between our pyramid of needs and the equipment to enable each level cannot be ignored. Each of the following sections addresses the matrix of our Hierarchy of Needs versus the gear required for the specific level of the pyramid.

Everyone has seen pictures of soldiers wearing harnesses and equipment. Modern day armies equip their troops with systems that look like dozens of pouches sewn onto a shirt, or vest. The military calls this category of gear **load-bearing equipment,** and it includes packs, pouches, and other items.

Soldiers break down their loads into three primary categories:

-> 1st Line – bare essentials to survive the day
-> 2nd Line - what is needed to execute the mission
-> 3rd Line – long-term survival needs

Preppers might describe these a little differently:

-> 1st Line – Basic stuff to survive
-> 2nd Line – Special gear to hide, infiltrate, evade, and scavenge
-> 3rd Line – Bug out bag

Unfortunately, the pyramid of needs does not correlate exactly to above-defined lines of gear. I believe the reason for this mismatch is that modern day armies depend on a sophisticated logistics system of supply. Given that most American troops are mounted in some way or another (Striker, Humvee, AAV, LAV-25, etc...) Thus, either their long-term survival needs (3rd line) are carried in their vehicle, or they can expect to be resupplied.

You will recall that during the Second Gulf War: Operation Iraqi Freedom (OIF), a halt was reported a few days after our troops crossed the border and began the invasion of Iraq. There were several headline stories of entire units not having enough food or other critical supplies, so advancement halted until the supply chain could catch up. This is not uncommon in warfare and has plagued every fast moving combat force since WWII.

Only Special Forces, Airborne and some none-direct combat units typically carry 3rd line equipment. This is one area where we preppers have a more difficult equipment situation than the typical soldier. Referring back to my family's bug out plan, our mount (my pickup truck) could be disabled, and we probably won't be able to radio for a recovery vehicle to come and get us. We won't have any resupply other than what we can fend for ourselves.

The actual alignment of equipment to needs is depicted in the chart below:

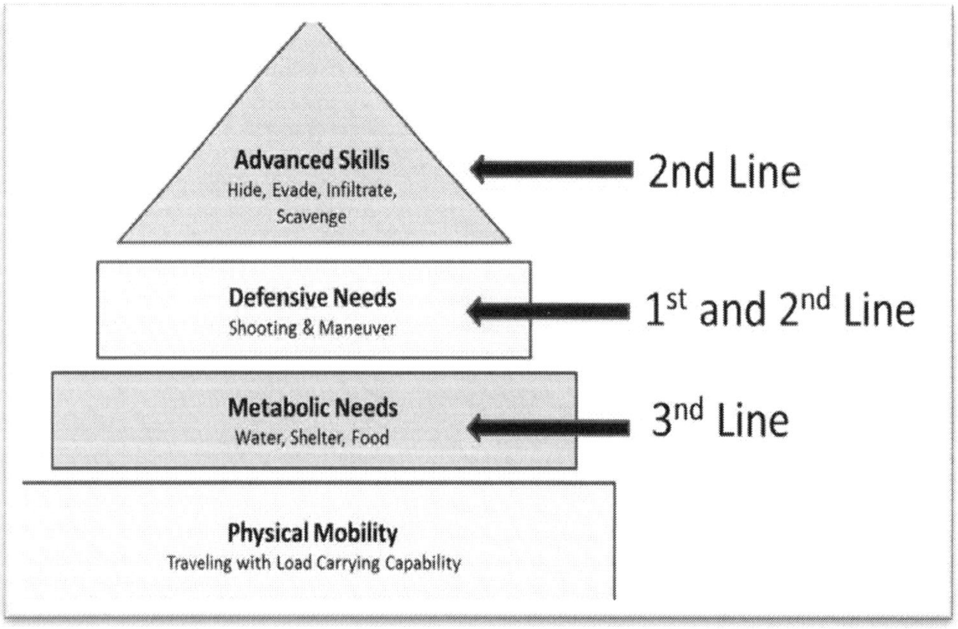

3.1 GEAR OF THE 1ST LINE

Our requirements for this load are the basic components necessary to "live through the day." This involves both defensive and some metabolic needs. An example of 1st line gear follows.

Example Chest-rig

A. Radio
B. Secondary (Pistol) with extra clip
C. Magazine for Rifle
D. Rifle maintenance kit and NVD
E. Medical Kit (blow out bag)
F. Dump pouch with rain coat, extra magazine, Jell-O and power bars
G. Knife
H. Flashlight

One of the first observations a combat veteran would make is our lack of ammunition as compared to a typical soldier. The example above would only have three rifle magazines (weapon, pouch and dump pouch), which is a small number as compared to a combat load.

We should take a moment and analyze the decision to limit ammunition. This example outlines the choices we may encounter post-SHTF. Weight is going to be our enemy, and ammo is heavy. If the goal for the day is to scavenge food, someone has to carry that loot back.

This discussion also emphasizes the need for planning. If our goal is to scout, other people must be avoided at all costs, so carrying a lot of ammo is just going to slow you down. If your mission involves a potential firefight, then carrying the extra rounds makes sense. The above load would have 84 rounds. Short of a pitched battle, that should be enough to break contact and skedaddle out of there. Keep in mind, the purpose is to survive – not defeat an organized enemy force.

Another common question is "why do you have Jell-O in your dump pouch?" Jell-O has a very high concentration of calories-to-weight/size. It has a good shelf life and is flexible in how it can be consumed. For example, if you mix it with water, it can help with the foul taste of some survival water sources.

The example above would be our equivalent to a soldier's 1st line gear - enough to keep a prepper in the fight, or to live for the day.

The map and compass (not shown) are in a zipper lining on the inside of the chest rig. A rear mounted water bladder provides hydration, and good optics on a rifle eliminates the need for binoculars.

While this may sound like a super heavy load, in reality it is not. Most people who don a MOLLE vest (or other load bearing system) for the first time are surprised at how much weight they can carry comfortably. The above list can be carried in just five pouches.

3.1.1 LINE ONE CHECKLIST

What you include with each line of gear is up to you. The conditions, terrain, and situation pertaining to the area of operations will dictate the three checklists. As you proceed through this book, the specialized equipment required for each task will round out your loads.

Operating in an urban or suburban environment will require a significantly different load-out than a remote desert area. The secret to determining a good balance between 1st and 3rd line gear is to practice.

As you determine what works for your situation and anticipated needs, you should utilize the least intrusive method of carrying the required equipment.

Here is my checklist for operating in a rural environment that surrounds my anticipated location. I had noted the justification (or lack thereof) for each item.

1st Line Contents	Justification
Knife	With a good knife you can do so many things.
Water Bladder	Never leave home without it.
Poncho	Like the knife above, a good poncho serves many tasks, not the least of which is keeping dry. My environment receives a lot of rain.
Jell-o and Powerbar	The highest density of calories to weight. Long shelf life. Cheap.
Night Vision Device	It is a game changer in any situation.
Paracord – 50 feet	Like the knife and poncho, this lightweight item is a multi-role no brainer.
First Aid Kit	You just never know. Really, this is difficult to justify in a non-combat role. I just feel better knowing it's there.
Weapon Maintenance Kit	Again, difficult to justify. Old habits die hard, and I want my weapon in tip top condition all the time.
Flashlight	Obvious, even with the night vision.
Compass and Map	Obvious, even with knowing the area well.
Spare Magazines	You never know when a mag is going to cause failure. Even if you are not expecting trouble, having spares makes sense.
Disposable Lighter	I am not a big fan of fire starting kits. A good lighter will function in all but the most extreme situations.

Many people would scoff at some of the items in the above list, especially if they intend to operate in an area with which they are familiar and close to their home. Some people may be tempted to adjust their load-out considering such parameters, but that may not be the best plan. Consider the example below, keeping in mind that my kit is based upon personal experience and is always being updated:

> A few months prior to this writing, I went to my bug out location (BOL) for the weekend. I wanted to do some weapons' training, walk the land, and generally get outdoors for a bit. My BOL is a remote Texas ranch, heavily wooded with good water and wildlife.

I noticed sign of ferial hogs in the area. These animals are destructive, and can be dangerous to people. Any hope of a garden, post SHTF, is a non-starter if these beasts are around. They will devour any natural food sources in the area as well. While some fresh pork would no doubt be welcome in a TEOTWAWKI life, hogs typically destroy food more than they produce. Additionally, these pests tend to become prolific and take over the area.

I decided to load up my 1st line gear, grab a rifle, and see if I could identify their number, size, and migration paths. I almost didn't take my gear. I was familiar with the land, had no intention of traveling more than a mile or so away from camp, and besides it was hot and muggy. "No, Mr. Joe Nobody," I said to myself, "Practice what you preach. Any time spent with your TEOTWAWKI gear is valuable."

I tracked the swine across the ranch's boundary and onto neighbor's land. I decided to pursue the herd because their number appeared to be sizeable. There is a standing agreement between the folks in this remote area granting cross-property rights – especially when hunting pests. While I knew the ranch well, I had only been on the neighbor's spread a few times.

I tracked the vermin for about 2 miles away from the ranch. The hogs were traveling parallel to a streambed, which had 15-foot steep banks. I needed to get to the other side, and found a tree that had fallen, making a handy natural bridge. This would keep my legs dry.

Midway through the crossing, the bridge collapsed, and I fell about 12 feet into the streambed. I landed on my side in about six inches of water. My body armor probably saved me a few broken ribs. As it were, my head cracked against a stone, and the breath was completely knocked out of me. A throbbing pain in my leg soon indicated I had twisted an ankle as well. The pain and swelling was increasing every minute.

My cell phone was crushed, not that there was anyone to call. The nearest help was three hours away at best. My instincts (and body) told me to stay put and recover. It wasn't long before I realized that one leg was quickly swelling, and I needed to head back to camp as soon as possible.

Now, I have a very good sense of natural direction. I seldom get turned around, but this day I did. After struggling up the bank, I headed off in what I thought was the route back to the ranch. Maybe it was the shock of the fall? Perhaps the pain was impacting my thinking? The reason why doesn't matter. I was limping away from my camp, not toward it.

In all of my adventures, I have carried a compass countless times and never used it. That day I did, and I was glad I had it. Did it save my life? No, unlikely. I would have eventually stumbled onto a farmhouse or road. What it did do is help me settle down and make it back to camp before I couldn't use my leg anymore or do additional damage to my body.

Did I need my body armor that day? Absolutely not, as the chances of a hunting accident were minimal. The odds of getting into a gunfight were next to none. But to this day, I believe that vest saved me from a serious injury. Had my landing driven a rib into a lung, the situation could have been much worse.

Did I need my weapon maintenance kit? No, I never fired a shot, nor did I have need to. My rifle had landed in the muddy sand without the barrel being fouled. A slightly different angle of fall, and I would have had to clean mud from the barrel. The thought of running into the hogs and being charged on the way home did cross my mind. Having my seldom-used maintenance kit provided me with comfort. It was good to know it was there.

Had I been unable to make it back to camp, I would have survived the night. I had the poncho for shelter or warmth and enough calories to keep my strength up. My medical kit contained some pain relief, should I have elected to use it. Again, it was reassuring to know it was there. While it sounds a little over-the-top now, at the time I was running through mental exercises and considering my options if my leg gave completely out and I might be stuck for several days.

Compared to many situations, this is not much of a survival story. I was really never in a life-threatening situation. If my physical situation had continued to deteriorate, I had the right equipment, and that helped my mindset. It is always a good idea to engineer equipment, carry system, and checklist with similar possibilities in mind.

EXERCISE

Make your 1st line gear checklist, and print it off. Cover it in a waterproof plastic cover, available at most office supply stores. Leave room to use a marker or grease pencil on the lamination so as to check items off before each undertaking. Store this checklist with your gear.

As we progress through more detailed planning in later chapters, this checklist will serve as a foundational item.

3.2 GEAR OF THE 2ND LINE

The purpose of 2nd line gear is to accomplish a specific objective. If our goal were to breach a medical building thought to have critical medications, we would carry our pry bar, bolt cutters or other specialized equipment in our 2nd line pack.

As most campers and hikers know, a problem with any **SIZE** backpack is **– its SIZE**. It seems the bag is always too large or too small for the next activity. Your carry system needs to address this issue. Hikers commonly go into a wilderness area with a heavy load, set up camp, and then take one or more day trips. Afterwards, they return to the primary camp. Several of the tactical actions described later will require a similar process.

Airborne Troopers use what is often referred to as an assault pack. This is basically a pack-within-a-pack arrangement. Heavy, overnight gear and longer-term non-essential supplies are left behind as the men move off to perform an action. They return later to retrieve their previously stored gear.

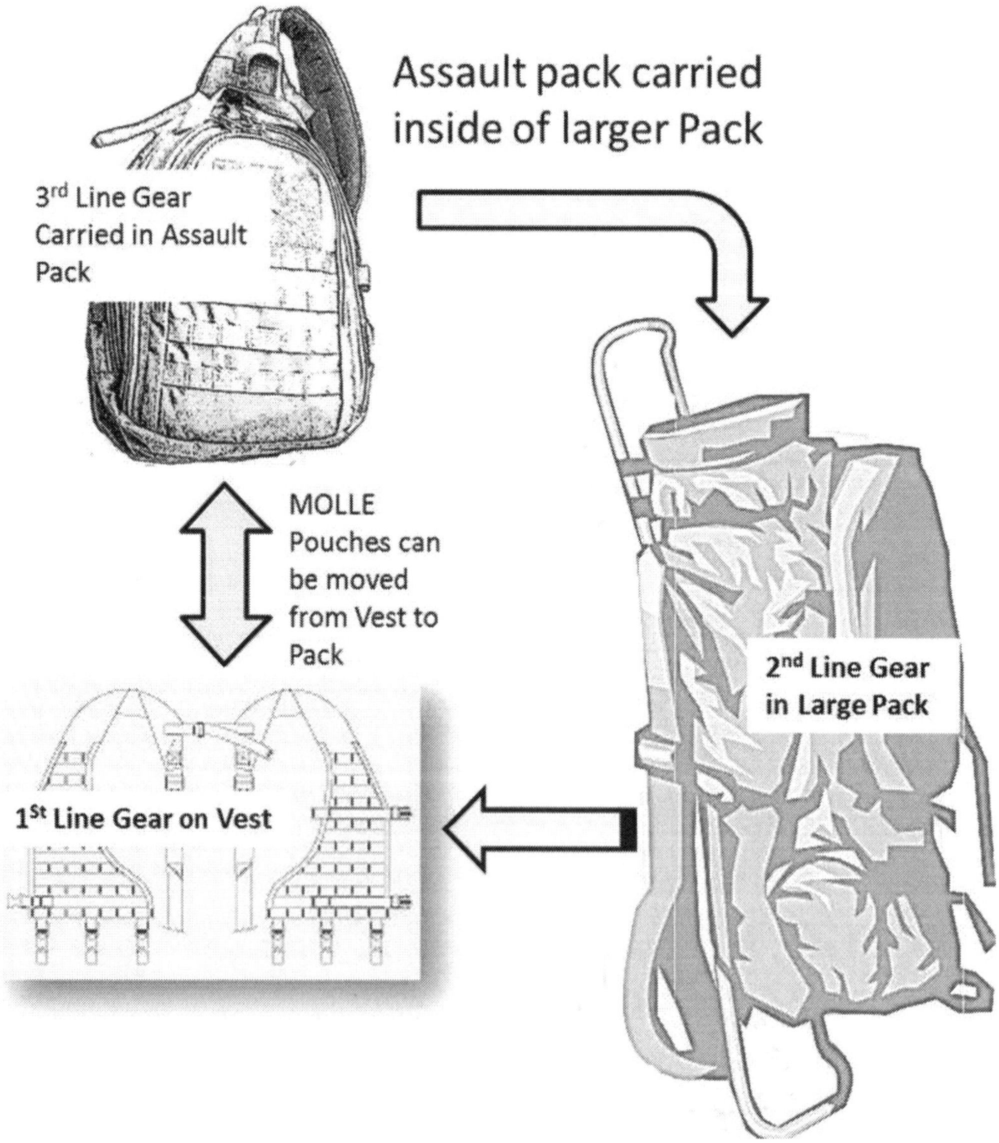

This example parallels our skills in several ways. Later, a scenario is described for infiltration that requires an overnight bivouac. Using the above method, the prepper might carry all of the required equipment to a nearby, concealed location and spend the night. During the infiltration, only the essential load would be included so as to reduce weight. After completing the infiltration, the gear left behind would be retrieved.

This is an important point when it comes to equipment selection. The 1st line gear should always be on your person in the form of a vest or chest rig. The 2nd and 3rd line equipment is going to be rearranged or reconfigured based on the next step of your objective. Using a smaller pack inside of your larger primary pack (next section) makes sense and is functional.

3.2.1 LINE TWO CHECKLIST

Since our 2nd Line gear will depend on our goal or assignment, each chapter addressing the four main skills will include a section on specialized equipment for that specific action. This list will typically be your line two checklist.

3.3 GEAR OF THE 3RD LINE

Given the size, weight, and requirements for 3rd line equipment, it is a safe assumption that a large camping backpack will be used. As preppers, our 3rd line gear involves longer-term metabolic needs. Shelter, water filtration, food preparations, and personal hygiene items are typical articles to be included here.

Like our 1st and 2nd line kits, the contents of your pack will depend on several factors. You will most likely need to:

- Spend the night in the field, perhaps more than one

- Prepare food

- Maintain equipment

- Prepare shelter

3.3.1 LINE THREE CHECKLIST

This is a simple list, and you should keep it that way. Below is my personal inventory of 3rd line gear:

- Mess kit and large metal cup with potholder.
- Silverware
- Water purifier
- Hoo-hahs (baby wipes) and assortment of plastic bags
- Shovel and spare tent stakes
- Rope
- Sleeping bag
- Spare clothes and socks
- Spices, medicine, 2 lighters and spare batteries
- Stove (WWII German Army model) and fuel
- Duct tape and fishing line
- Rain poncho (make sure it will fit over the pack)
- Hatchet and glow sticks
- Food
- Microfiber towels (2)
- Soap, insect repellant, and sunscreen

With the above list, I can survive for several days without resupply. Using the scenario of my family's bug out and the loss of our truck, we each have our own packs.

Your specific gear will also depend on your general environment. Cold weather makes a big difference in 3rd Line contents. Rural versus urban areas will also have an impact. Your area of operation (AO) will dictate many differences. As an example, my primary AO has plentiful sources of water. I don't pack as much water as I would if operating in a desert environment because I can always find water and filter it. Were my primary AO be in an area where water was scarce, I would adjust the contents of my pack. Another option involves the tent/sleeping bag combination versus a hammock. Personally, I believe a hammock is always the better night's rest. You need trees (or other structure) to hang the hammock from. If my primary AO was the high plains, a tent/sleeping bag would be mandatory because there is often nothing to hang the hammock on.

EXERCISE

Make your 3rd line gear checklist, and print it off. Cover it in a waterproof plastic cover, available at most office supply stores. Leave room to use a marker or grease pencil on the lamination so as to check items off before each mission. Store this checklist with your gear.

As you progress through the following chapters, detailed plans and exercises will be created. All of the example simulations and rehearsals will require the foundational capabilities described above. As you work with your load-bearing equipment and the contents, you should create equipment checklists and timelines.

EXERCISE

The following actions are typical metabolic activities:

(1) Prepare a meal
- a. Stove
- b. Open fire

(2) Set up a bivouac
- a. Shelter
- b. Sleeping area

(3) Using the restroom
(4) Break camp
(5) Refill or filter water

For each of these items, you need to know how long each task takes and what equipment is required. This information will be required in later exercises. As you practice these actions, time yourself and make a detailed inventory list of what exactly was used. If operating alone, film yourself and review later. The equipment being used should be cross-referenced using the equipment lists created in the above sections on *Line One Checklist* and *Gear of the 3rd Line*.

Military snipers record detailed information about their rifles, weather conditions, and specific ammunition. This is often called **DOPE**, or Data on Previous Engagements.

You, as a prepper, need to have the DOPE on your camping skills. Later, when strict timelines are required, the time spent setting up a bivouac will be important to know. Good operational planning works on a strict timeline. If you are going to scout a potentially hostile location, you want to be in place and well hidden before dawn. How can you stay on a schedule if you don't know how long it takes to break camp, pack up your gear, and get moving?

The following is an example of how to record your time intervals and equipment:

Task	Total Time	Equipment Used
Prepare a meal – stove	18 minutes	Stove Fuel Mess Kit Utensils Water Cup Lighter Towel Spices Food
Prepare Meal – open fire	22 minutes	Ax Fuel Mess Kit Utensils Water Cup Lighter Towel Spices Food
Prepare Meal – cold	14 minutes	Fuel Mess Kit Utensils Water Cup Lighter Towel Spices Food
Tent Bivouac	19 minutes	Tent Sleeping bag
Hammock Bivouac	18 minutes	Rope

4. TRAINING WITH YOUR KIT

The best way to train with your equipment is to have access to private land that can be used to hunt or walk for extended periods. Climbing fences, jumping creeks, ascending hills and wandering through valleys will quickly indicate how well your system is working. Of course, the more physically fit someone is, the easier this will be.

4.1 WORKOUTS

A cardinal rule among military professionals is:

TRAIN HOW YOU WILL FIGHT

For those of us who prepare, I recommend a motto of:

TRAIN HOW YOU WILL LIVE

For preppers, training takes on a slightly different meaning when compared to the typical soldier. Most preppers are older and have regular daily activates like jobs, children, hobbies or other duties. They cannot engage in maneuvers, exercises and drills like a full time soldier or Marine.

However, there are several methods of training that can be performed by the average person. These exercises will serve to prepare everyone should a critical need suddenly arise. The knowledge and experience of how to properly use and carry your gear should not be left to the last minute, as it may be too late to implement corrections.

EXERCISE

The first order of business, after acquiring any gear, is to balance the loads. Since load-bearing systems are shoulder based, it would be prudent to pack everything up, strap on a rifle and walk around the house. *While the wife and kids may think you are a little "touched," the teasing now will be less painful than sore shoulders and blisters later.* The goal is to achieve balance. Make sure that the gear is balanced left to right or side-to-side. *You also can extract revenge by having everyone test his or her loads as well.*

The second task is to verify everything can be reached as you carry it. Can the spare clips be pulled out? Can the secondary (pistol) be drawn without it becoming snagged? Do the spare rifle magazines come out ready to be inserted (rather than flipped around) into the rifle?

The third task is to make sure everything is comfortable moving into a shooting position with a rifle. Does your weapon's sling get hung up on a pouch? Does it feel good on the shoulder and allow a proper cheek weld?

While checking the rifle, make **SURE** that a transition to the pistol can be executed well. There is no need to be Wild West gunslinger quick – smooth is fast under stress. Also, can the spare clips for the pistol be easily accessed?

The last item to verify is that walking is comfortable with the full load. You need to know that everything works before the SHTF. If a fix requires different equipment, you may not be able to run down to the store and purchase what you need. Some problems don't show themselves immediately:

Not long ago, I decided to try high capacity magazines for my 1911 pistol. Having those extra two rounds seemed like a good idea at the time. I utilize a standard belt-mounted holster. Only after wearing the rig for a day did I found they (the extended mags) weren't going to work for me. The combination of my holster, belt and carry position caused the extended tip of the magazine to rub a hole through my pants. Another day of carry would have surely produced some raw skin.

My profession requires that I constantly evaluate gear. Over the years, I have developed a routine to see if a new piece of kit is going to work for me. Here is the process I have used as I prepare:

1) I put everything on at once. A new holster may feel good in the store, but may result in having an unreachable pistol after being adjusted for body armor and load vest. Take the time and put it ***all*** on.

2) Wearing full gear, I do what I would normally do around the house. Reloading, cleaning weapons, hanging clean clothes, and all of my normal tasks are performed wearing my kit. If you can't fold the laundry wearing your rig, how do you expect to be able to evade pursuit?

3) I walk – a lot. I carry my stuff around the ranch and make sure I do everything from cross creeks to climb fences. I go up hill and down, through dense underbrush and open pasture. Nothing will prove the serviceability of your gear more than wearing it all day. This is good exercise as well.

4) I go prone with my gear on. A gunfight is bad time to determine that pouch on the front of your vest digs into your ribs so bad you can't breathe while on your belly.

5) I run with my gear on. Again, discovering that your sling slams into your testicles, while running away from hostiles, shows a great lack of planning.

I have lost count of the number of times I have seen men show up at rifle classes wearing brand new load gear, anxious to try out their new duds. Halfway through the first day, they are complaining of blisters, asking for Band-Aids, and constantly readjusting rigs. By the end of a three-day class, many of them are showing up with much less equipment than they started with.

If the class involves an obstacle course, it is an amazing sight to see the pouches, magazines, knives and other gear scattered around on the ground after the class runs the gauntlet. The instructors often call these people "litterbugs."

There is no excuse for having load equipment that doesn't function. Obviously, you wanted the kit. You went out and spent hard-earned money on it. Put it on and work out the kinks.

Once everything is comfortable and secure, the next step is creating ways to train with your gear.

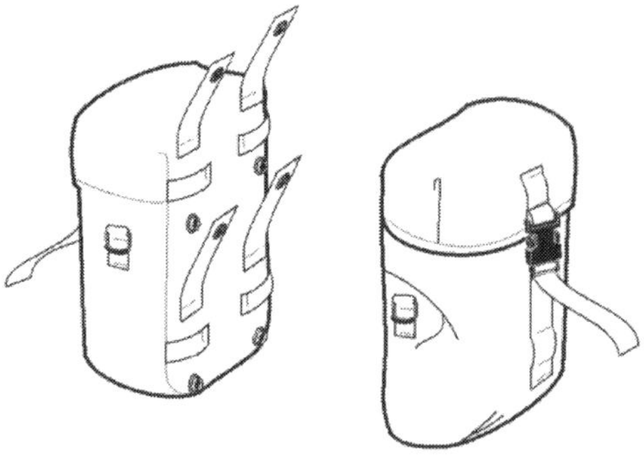

EXERCISE

Even if your equipment functions perfectly, it won't do you much good if you can't carry it for extended periods of time. The physical fitness part of survival cannot be overlooked. This is not to say that you have to be at the same level of conditioning as a Navy SEAL. There is no requirement to carry logs over your head in soft sand for miles.

On the other hand, you are not going to be able to scavenge if you can't walk to and from the target. The best gauge of usability is to put your gear on and walk the countryside. If taking your equipment to somewhere private is not an option, then the next best thing is using a weight vest. These are available at almost any sporting goods store and are used by athletes to perform endurance training. They have 12-20 small, sewn in pouches that contain removable sand bags. The weight can be adjusted by removing or adding the little sand bags and thus gradually increasing the weight load over time. These are flat, non-military looking vests and can be covered up with a sweatshirt or loose jacket. Simply go for a walk around the neighborhood. No one will know that a secret training program to become a MOLLE equipped operator is in progress. The exercise will increase your endurance regardless.

I also believe in loading up all of my gear and going up and down the stairs a few times. Even an active person will be surprised at the effort this takes.

For the average prepper, there is no need to be able to pass a military fitness test while wearing full gear. The most important capability is to be able to walk reasonable distances.

My full chest rig weighs less than 14 pounds fully loaded with secondary weapon. Many business executives commonly carry a computer bag, cell phone, wallet, car keys, and bottle of water. All of this civilian gear would be just a few pounds less. Folks routinely walk through airports, parking garages and to meetings carrying almost identical weight.

The average lady's purse can't be far behind in the weight category. If an umbrella or raincoat is added, the weight is almost equal.

For the 2nd and 3rd line gear, the absolute best way to train is to camp and hike while wearing the gear. There is no need to wear the military looking MOLLE vest and frighten all the hikers and rangers. This is another reason why it may be prudent to select a non-military backpack. It can be worn anywhere without issue. While carrying a rifle is out of the question (unless on private land), any option to become familiar with the weight of the equipment is a positive.

If a bicycle is part of the plan for TEOTWAWKI transportation, ride it with the pack on. Make sure it does not stress back muscles or interfere with balance, braking, or other actions.

The same applies to a horse or any other method of transportation.

For elderly folks, or those who have a physical limitation, a common golf bag caddy may be an option. These little hand pulled carts are typically robust and designed to carry a lot of weight. They are very inexpensive, and a good size backpack would fit perfectly on one.

4.2 PERSONALITY CONFLICTS WITH YOUR KIT

No system is perfect, and there will always be adjustments to be made. Once everything is fully connected, loaded, and practiced, the load can remain uncomfortable and "disagreements" are common. Don't give up! There are several options available to resolve these situations.

A common issue with any kit is having the rifle magazine sticking out from the body of the rifle and becoming entangled with the pouches at your mid-section. An AR15's (or any magazine fed weapon) 30 round mag takes up a lot of space and extends below the rifle a few inches. It can get hung up on gear, bang body parts, and cause general mayhem. One idea is to carry a 10 round magazine (much shorter) in the rifle when not expecting trouble. This alternative is smaller and less intrusive. It can also be carried on the vest or chest rig to reduce weight.

Most rigs are very adjustable; and having someone else to pull straps, tighten buckles and generally custom fit the rig to your individual shape can help.

There are under-load-bearing-equipment tops called compression shirts that have padding where the typical load weight rests and rubs. These shirts can make a tremendous difference.

Finally, weight can be reduced in several ways. If the rifle carries comfortably, mount a flashlight on the rifle rather than on your base vest or rig. The same can be done with night vision or NVD.

Examine every single component and see if a lighter piece of equipment is available. Many times, a weight saving unit that will perform the same function is an option. *I recently discovered an ultra-lightweight rifle cleaning kit that reduced weight.*

Again, the military professionals have a saying:

Ounces = Pounds and Pounds = Pain

Even if a different equipment option only saves a few ounces, it will all add up. Always be on the lookout for lighter gear even if your kit is already comfortable. If nothing else, carrying more food or water could be important if additional weight capacity is available.

5. THE SURVIVAL NET

One of the most versatile pieces of equipment available is a survival net. With perhaps the exception of a good knife, I can't think of a more valuable piece of post-SHTF gear.

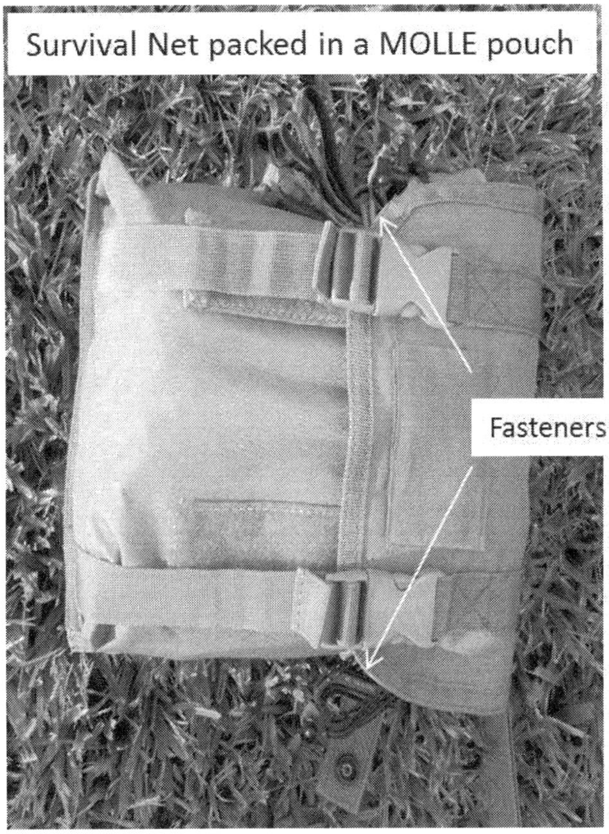

Survival Nets can be used as:
Ghillie Suit
Ghillie Hide
Ghillie Blanket
Hammock
Looters bag
Stretcher
Fishing Net
Climbing Tool
Trap
Snare
Emergency Shelter
Emergency Coat or Blanket
Emergency Raft or Float
Door or Window Security
Cargo Net

A good net system is lightweight, robust and can make the difference between life and death. The system involves more than just a mesh of nylon; it includes fasteners, supports and of course, some basic skills.

A workable survival net is made from materials that are both weather resistant and strong enough to support realistic weights. If you are going to be using the system for ghillie camouflage, then the "squares" should be less than one inch so that foliage can be securely weaved into place.

The net's break weight should be at least 250 pounds if it will serve as a hammock or climbing tool. If you are a large individual, you want a little stronger mesh as you should count the weight of your equipment when determining the required strength of the net. Keep in mind the higher the tensile rating, the heavier the net.

Another key feature to a good net system is the supports. Malleable aluminum splints can be molded into various shapes and weigh less than six ounces. Besides the obvious medical uses, they have numerous secondary roles, and one manufacturer even claims they have been used as a makeshift paddle for a raft. Another option is re-usable equipment ties. These come in many different lengths. I would recommend at least 18 inches in length to be usable with the net.

Supports are used to stabilize the net as it is being used in different roles. An example benefit would be the ability to form an irregular shape, which most experts agree is critical to effective camouflage.

Fasteners are the final component of a good net system. Fine quality climbing "S" hooks are versatile and strong. For some uses, common rubber bands work well. Nylon tie strips can also be handy as they are strong and light.

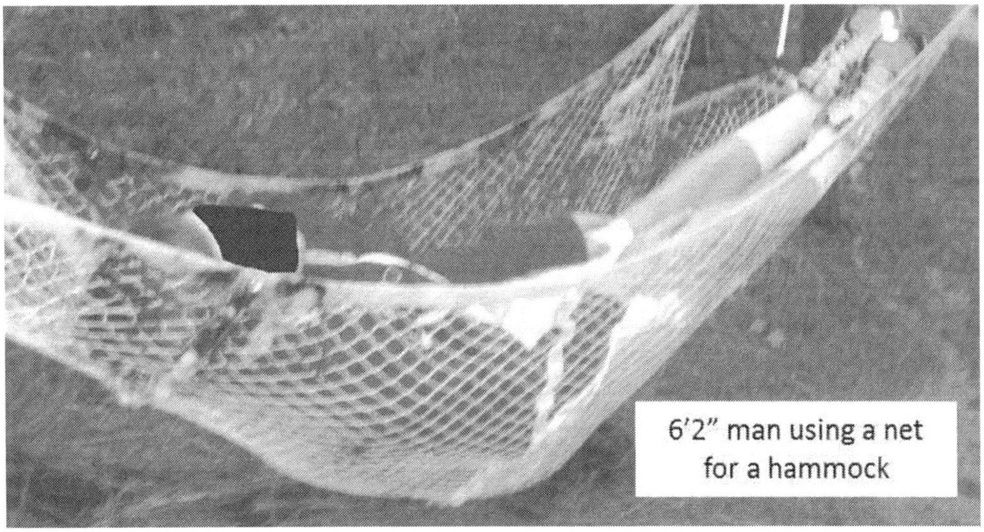

6’2” man using a net for a hammock

In the following chapters, we will use a survival net many times. Prepare with a good system of netting – it may save your life.

6. PRIMARY WEAPONS

It is unlikely you will require any of the skills in this book unless your environment becomes violent. There should be no need to hide, evade, or infiltrate if the world is a tranquil place. Since most of us live in areas where violent crime already exists, it is probably naive to believe a collapse of society will improve the situation.

I personally use an M4 Carbine, which is basically an AR15 with a few minor modifications. In reality, any weapon that delivers enough firepower and can be either folded or stored in less than 24-26 inches is preferable as a primary weapon. Some other examples of firearms in this category would be:

- FN SCAR (with folding stock)
- Remington Adaptive Combat Rifle (ACR) – Enhanced with folding stock
- AK47 (with folding stock)
- Mini-14 (with folding stock)

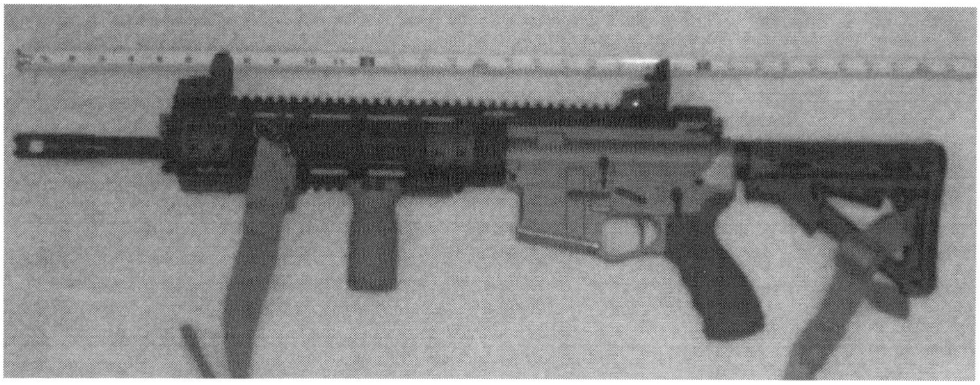

For those who use an AR15 as their primary "go to" weapon, verify the length when the weapon is broken down (lower separated from the upper). There are hundreds of manuals and websites addressing the breaking down of an AR, so I will not repeat the process here. It is very simple, and in a matter of seconds, you can shorten the length of the weapon significantly.

The broken down rifle is now 24 inches long. We can hide or carry this rifle in more concealed positions or containers than the fully assembled weapon. If you have the proper tax stamp and local laws allow, you can accomplish the same goal by purchasing a short-barreled rifle (SBR). I, personally, am not a big fan of SBRs, but many professionals recommend them in certain situations.

If you are going to use a "normal" AR15 and need to break it down, you should secure the bolt carrier group in some fashion. I have found a common rubber band does the trick quite well. If I have to put the rifle together in a hurry, an elastic band is easier to remove than duct tape or other devices.

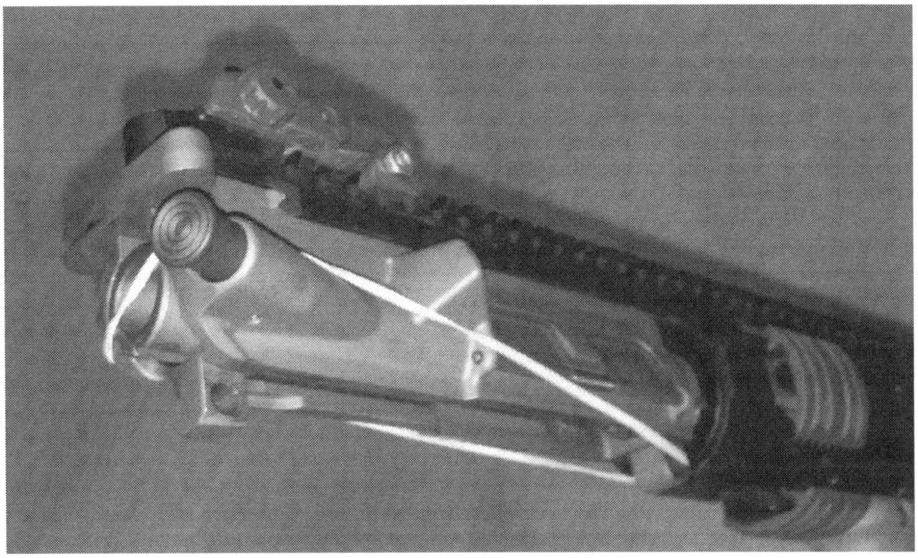

In today's world, it is rare that a short weapon is required. Few typical actions, military or civilian, require such compact storage of a long gun. One group that commonly uses shorter length carbines or sub-machine guns would be the Special Forces. Those operators have a wide inventory of weapons to choose from and can select a weapon that meets their exact requirements. If they need a compact weapon, they can switch from their normal battle rifle to something more exotic. We preppers probably won't have that option (unless you have a great gun safe fully stocked) and will have to go with our everyday survival weapon.

Choosing a weapon for survival can be a complex process. Most weapons are dedicated to a specific use, such as hunting, fighting, training, target shooting, or others. Weapons (guns) are like automobiles or practically anything else – **they are a compromise**. In the case of weapons, the compromises are between weight, power, reliability, cost, availability of ammo, and all sorts of other factors.

This book addresses advanced survival skills that are certainly not "typical." One of the reasons why I choose an AR15 platform weapon is its flexibility. I can quickly configure my blaster in the field and use it to fulfill several roles.

So what is the perfect weapon for survival? **There is no perfect weapon for survival or any other use.** The choice depends on skill level, budget, and projected needs. If in an urban area, then a weapon designed for anti-personal usage, like an AK74 or similar may be a good choice.

Any rifle is a machine, and like all machines, they can break or fail. There are a couple of sayings that should be taken seriously when it comes to weapons:

"**Buy nice or buy twice**" is really true. For the most part, you get what you pay for in a weapon. In our market-driven economy, there are too many manufacturers in competition for the consumer dollar for comparable products to be overpriced for long. Will a $1,000 rifle shoot better or last longer than a $2,000 dollar rifle of a similar platform – not likely.

This rule holds true until you start getting into the exotic big game or hunting rifles. Some of these "works of art" go for tens of thousands of dollars and are worth it to their specialized market. *I would not invest in one of these types of rifles for a defense weapon, long range, or medium range.*

"**One is none – Two is one**" is another old adage that really rings true. Even the highest quality, well-maintained weapons can jam or break. What is intended by this wisdom is that you need a backup weapon. Most professional soldiers refer to this as a secondary, and most people normally choose a pistol. I apply the 1=0, 2=1 rule differently as a prepper in that I am not sure my local gunsmith will be around to fix my broken weapons. Therefore, I keep clones of all of my weapons for spare parts as well as extras of critical parts in my kit.

6.1 PERSONAL OPTICS

Most anyone who spends time in the field knows the value of magnification. Example tools include binoculars, riflescopes, range finders and any other number of devices that increase the capability to see at distance. For a survival situation, having this capability may be critical. For the primary subjects contained in this book, the role of optics is even more important. In the chapter on infiltration, there is an in-depth section on reconnaissance. Years ago, being able to scout a target from a distance would have required carrying binoculars and a riflescope. With modern technology, you can leave the heavy binoculars at home and save the weight.

6.2 OFFSET MOUNTS

In later chapters, the need to scout, inspect or gather intelligence on a distant location will be required. As described above, the weight of our equipment is going to be a constant concern. One method to reduce your carry weight is to use a powerful rifle optic in place of binoculars. This method does have a few shortcomings, however. First of all, a large optic greatly reduces the weapon's capabilities close in. You just can't acquire targets that are "danger close" with a big scope. One solution is to equip your big optic with an offset mount. An offset mount allows for both a large magnification riflescope and a holographic red dot to be mounted on a rifle at the same time. As shown below, a small red dot is attached to the riflescope with a mount. This enhancement will not harm a good, quality scope.

This option allows for a very high-powered riflescope for long distance observation AND shooting, as well as a close in, fast acquisition optic. The small, holographic red dot weighs just a few ounces and is very effective.

Our second shortcoming is that a riflescope does not provide nearly the field of view when compared to a good pair of binoculars. While it is common to have much more magnification with a modern scope, you can't see nearly as much ground as with a dedicated set of binoculars.

6.3 NIGHT VISION

There is a lot of equipment you can purchase to improve your defensive capabilities. Probably the biggest game changer I have ever spent money on is night vision.

In Afghanistan, not many years ago, it was more difficult to obtain government permits for night vision and body armor than select fire (full automatic) weapons. This policy, no doubt, was influenced by United States military. Commanders fully understand the advantage this technology provides, and every step is taken to keep these devices out of enemy hands.

Even today, U. S. export of NVDs is strictly prohibited.

A night vision device is rated in Generations, with Gen 1, 2, 3 or 4 being currently available. The price goes up with higher generations.

In addition to the generation of the device, you also need to verify that it is gated, which means it can withstand bright lights, like the muzzle flash of a weapon, without damage.

NVDs come in several different configurations. You can purchase dedicated weapon sights, goggles, and monocles. I have found that the monocles are the most useful in that you can mount them on an AR15 in front of your normal optics (if you purchase compatible optics), as well as use them stand-alone.

Some people like to mount NVD on their rifles, while others like a head mount or helmet mount system.

In addition, you will need to configure your MOLLE load-bearing equipment to handle the weight and storage of your NVD.

The typical device is not heavy, but NVD goggles can be bulky. Any type of head mount will also be a bulky storage problem for MOLLE.

A Generation 3 NVD is so effective you can drive safely, at night without headlights. I can also hunt effectively at night, and that could be important in a post-event environment. NVD **will not** see through smoke or fog. Infrared is designed for that capability.

Unless your foe has NVD, you will own the night. And remember, on average, we will spend one third of our time on this earth in low or no light conditions.

As of this writing, a quality Gen-3 Monocle, such as a PVS-14, is about $2900. That is a lot of cash, but again, I can't think of a single item you can purchase for the same money that will improve your capabilities as much as NVD.

In the last few years, Forward Looking Infrared (**FLIR**) devices have become available to the general public. These units are extremely expensive, ranging from $6,000 to over $25,000. FLIR devices give the added advantage over simple NVD of being able to see through smoke and some amounts of fog. Personally, I can't justify the expense for my intended purposes. I keep an eye on the prices as they continue to decline. When FLIR technology approaches the price of existing light gathering NVD, then I will probably consider a purchase, but not before then.

NOTE- NVDs are battery powered. Most take standard sizes, such as AA, so a rechargeable is a valid option.

7. HOW TO HIDE

The first advanced skill to be addressed is how to hide.

Most of us played hide and seek as children. In a survival situation, being able to properly conceal yourself is more than just a child's game. It may be the difference between life and death. There are countless situations where this skill can be applied:

- Avoiding capture or pursuit
- Egress or retreat
- Scouting or reconnaissance
- Staging an ambush

The other topics contained in this book utilize hiding, or concealment, to varying degrees. If you are trying to **evade** others, knowing how to hide may become critical. If you need to **scavenge** in a populated area, being able to conceal yourself may be the difference between replenishing your supplies and being target practice.

7.1 SPECIAL EQUIPMENT

- Shovel
- Machete, knife or ax
- Survival net
- Ghillie raw materials to fit the environment
- Rope
- Fasteners (safety pins, paper clips, rubber bands, etc.)

7.2 OBSERVATION

Before delving into specifics on hiding, the art of observation has to be addressed. Understanding how people look at things is important for two reasons:

1. You want to be able to select a quality hiding position. You may not have a lot of time to make a choice. Being a good observer will increase your chances of finding the best place to hide.
2. Your choice of a position should be based on how the people you are hiding from will observe the area. This knowledge allows you to make a better decision, decreasing your chances of being discovered.

Most self-defense experts teach that being **aware** of your surroundings is the most important aspect of avoiding trouble. If you are *aware* of someone following you, the attacker will lose the element of surprise. If you are *aware* of the three thugs ahead of you at the corner, and cross the street before passing them, they have more difficulty accosting you. It's no different when it comes to concealment. Developing a keen eye and observing the territory, people, structures and plant life in your area is critical to avoiding discovery. The example that follows shows a wooded landscape.

Even though our image is in black and white, you can learn a lot about observation by studying this picture. Try the following:

Look away from the picture for a moment, and then look back taking note of where your eyes focus first. Most people will initially focus on the pathway along the left side of the image, followed by the open area in the center (behind the closest tree). Your brain will travel to the open areas first because it is lazy. The open areas have less detail, and thus offer a visual path of least resistance. Your brain wants as much information as it can get while expending as little effort as possible.

After the open areas, the typical person will visually inventory the darkest areas next. Black is not a common color in nature, and our brains have registered this fact over the years. Darwin would probably have attributed this habit to survival of the fittest, seeking the potential threat in the shadows, as outlined in the picture below.

The last place our eyes would naturally travel would be the dense, highly detailed brush. Again, our eyes are lazy and want to provide as much input using the least amount of effort. Studying thick foliage and discerning the detail of individual leaves and branches requires our brains to expend more energy.

Have you have ever heard the phrase "a trained observer"? Often police officers receive observation training, which essentially involves forcing their eyes to focus on detail. This type of training disciplines the mind to take a photographic image of the objects, area, or target. Recalling details about that mental image allows for accurate observation.

Military snipers are taught photographic recall to an extreme level. Often in their training, a group of random objects is placed on a table. Objects such as a paper clip, ink pen, car keys, or apple are spread out, and the students are given a short amount of time to look them over. Later, they are asked to recall and describe all of the items. As their training progresses, the number of objects increases while the observation time is reduced. The time between observation and recall is also increased. They are shown the table full of objects in the morning, and then asked to recall late in the day.

EXERCISE

Try this game to improve your observation skills:

- Have a friend place random objects in your backyard or other area while you are not looking. Everyday objects that would commonly be seen in the area should be used. Lawn chairs, ball, hose ... etc.

- Once everything is in place, attempt to take a mental snapshot of the area. I normally use the corner of the house and poke my head around as if I expect someone to shoot at me. Make the observation quickly.

- Take a piece of paper and draw each object and its location.

- Try increasing the number of objects.

- Try placing an object that would be completely out of place in the area. An example would be can of soup in the backyard.

- Try having someone walk through the area as you take your mental snapshot.

If you really want to train, put on some safety gear, and have someone shoot a paintball or plastic BBs at you when you poke your head around the corner. Even having a friend throw a tennis ball at your head as you try to observe is useful.

It is only common sense that as the number of objects increases, your accuracy in recalling them will decrease. If you practice several times, however, you will be surprised at how quickly you can improve. You should also notice that the unusual object draws your attention away from the common or expected objects. The same can be said of the person walking, as the human eye is drawn to movement.

This exercise has two benefits:

(1) If you know how observation works, you can select a better hiding place.

(2) Scouting, or performing reconnaissance, may be a valuable skill in a post-collapse life. In a later chapter, we will cover how learning to quickly observe, note and document details could improve your chances of survival.

As children, many of us enjoyed games that involved finding objects that "didn't belong" in a picture or drawing. These games equate to basic observation training. If you are hiding, you don't want to be what is wrong, or stand out in any way. Knowing how any observer's mind works can help you accomplish this goal.

In summary, the combination of "where someone will look" combined with "not appearing unusual or out of place" is critical to hiding. If we know the brain will avoid detail, and we learn to blend in, then our chances of being observed are decreased.

Affective concealment, or hiding, is dependent upon four separate aspects:

(1) Position

(2) Movement discipline

(3) Noise discipline

(4) Camouflage or disguise

7.3 POSITION

Selecting a good position depends on the objective, or the reason why you need to hide. If you want to recon a location for potential scavenging, you need a clear view. If you are trying to hide from an adversary, then possible escape routes should influence your selection.

Practically any position is a compromise. In the field, perfect hiding spots are rare.

The resources at your disposal will also influence the choice of a position. If I am wearing a deep woods ghillie suit while trying to hide in an urban area, I don't have the proper resources. A guy wearing a tuxedo can't hide on a beach.

Another factor to consider is how long you will have to maintain the position. Movement discipline overlaps with this decision point, as most people cannot remain in an awkward stance for long periods without muscle cramps or discomfort. If a position requires standing, sitting, squatting, or lying prone, your physical condition and comfort should be part of the selection process.

7.3.1 WHERE NO MAN HAS GONE BEFORE

One of the most commonly overlooked criteria when selecting a hiding position is human adversity. People naturally dislike bad smells, damp or moldy areas, and mud. It is only human nature to avoid garbage dumps, trash heaps and other smelly areas. The smell of sewage is another example.

In wooded terrain, it is a little more difficult to find areas that invoke adversity. A ripe, large, dead animal may cause some people to avoid getting too close, while others may be curious. Muddy areas are commonly avoided by passersby, if at all possible.

This is an area where mental attitude and discipline separate the highly skilled and motivated from the average person.

In a post-collapse urban area, it is reasonable to assume there will be smelly, larva infested trash heaps. These "avoid at all costs" eyesores exist today in some cities. If your life is on the line, could you disguise yourself and hide in the trash heap? Could you stay there for hours? In Iraq, military snipers used some of the most disgusting places to hide imaginable. They wanted to set up in a position where their odds of being discovered were the lowest.

Could you hide under a dead, rotting horse carcass? How about a termite infested log or a fresh manure heap at a farm?

There are countless places that people naturally have an instinct to avoid. Hiding where no one else wants to go simply makes sense. Among survival experts, common wisdom states, "You will be surprised at what you will eat if hungry enough." Will you be surprised at where you will hide your body if desperate enough?

When I was a young lad, my friends and I played a form of hide-and-seek in nearby woods. One memorable afternoon, a skunk had used its spray for some unknown reason. I was surrounded and soon to be discovered by my buddies. Having no option, I took cover right in the middle of the horrible odor. My foes approached, smelled the skunk, and avoided the area. Later, no one wanted to be around me for some reason, but winning the game that day was worth it.

Here are some tips for adapting to undesirable hiding areas.

Odor is one of the most potent sensory inputs when it comes to the attractiveness of an area. Nothing broadcasts a stronger stay away signal than a rank smell. Many people spend their entire working day in environments that most of us would find incredibly offensive. "You get used to it," is a common philosophy. A prepper hiding in brackish swamp water may not have the time to get acclimated to it, and yet still must focus on survival and not the bad smell.

-You can overcome bad scents by applying a small amount of vapor rub, muscle cream or even wild peppermint under your nose. If you are wearing a mask, try rubbing a dab of pinesap in the area just above your lips. It can work wonders.

-Simply breathing through paper filters can help with some offensive aromas.

-Chewing a strong breath mint or gum works for a short period of time.

The expression, "That makes my skin crawl," is an adept description of some good hiding places. I can't count the number of times I have gone prone and found myself visited by crawling insects. In southern climates, fire ants can be a serious concern. These vicious creatures can kill with their swarming bites and should obviously be avoided.

Other than a few exceptions, most "crawlies" are harmless irritants. Even the biters will leave you alone unless movement causes them to feel threatened. You shouldn't be moving anyway.

Again, a few lessons learned over the years concerning our multi-legged friends:

- Tuck your pants into your boots - it helps. If this is uncomfortable, buy extra-long shoelaces, and tie the additional length around the cuffs. This works almost as well. The military issues what is called blousing rubbers or blousing straps, which are essentially big rubber bands with hooks at each end. They are used to blouse your pants above your boots. Anything that seals the trouser legs, even a rubber band or nylon tie will work.

- Long sleeve shirts will provide some protective barrier as well.

- A shirt (blouse) that can be buttoned tightly around the neck is effective. If your long-term comfort is a consideration, try and remember the last time you had to wear a shirt and tie for the day.

- Gloves provide a physical and mental barrier to unpleasant tactile sensations. One word of advice – most gloves are made from materials that harbor bacteria. Just like your hands, you should wash or disinfect your gloves if they have been in contact with substances carrying deadly germs, such as human waste or rotting flesh.

Damp or moist areas, such as swamps or backwaters, can be excellent hiding places. The courage to lie in such areas can be difficult to muster, especially if in a region where poisonous snakes or other dangerous wildlife exists. Most wildlife will not bother you if you don't move. Years ago, I fell asleep sitting with my back against a tree. A strange sensation caused me to wake, only to find an 8-foot black snake crawling across my legs. While not a dangerous animal, I froze, and the reptile continued on with its business, never giving me a second glance. Had I been in a survival situation, he might have been dinner.

The point is that humans are simply not natural prey for most creatures. If you are motionless, thus non-threatening, most critters will leave you alone. Even scorpions and spiders will seldom attack unless frightened. Television programs featuring zoologists who allow tarantulas to crawl up and down their arms are a prime example of this fact.

Not all wildlife should be dismissed as docile. Alligators are a serious concern in some areas. When it comes to 'gators, you are on your own – avoid them. Rare areas of the U.S. are still inhabited by big cats, such as mountain lions. Bears, wolves and other large predators may also be a serious threat in your region. Most people who live in proximity to these animals already have local knowledge on how to stay on top of the food chain. In most situations, larger animals will stay in remote areas, so using your noisy weapon as a last resort may be your only option. It may also result in a good meal.

7.3.2 SMOKE SIGNALS

Hunters have used smoke baths for hundreds of years. If you are unfamiliar with the concept, a smoke bath involves setting a very small fire that generates a lot of smoke. The bather stands over the fire (or downwind) and basically lets the smoke drift over his or her body. To tolerate the burning smoke, bathers hold their breath and close their eyes.

Anyone who has ever cooked marshmallows on a stick over a campfire has probably taken a smoke bath. For those who camp often, the smell of smoke permeating clothing is well known.

The smoke fragrance on your skin and clothing does much more than mask the human scent when hunting. Insects, as well as most animals, don't like the smell of smoke. A good smoke bath has been known to deter even the most ferocious mosquitoes.

A smoke bath, or other scent reduction technique, is a multi-purpose activity. Not only will it discourage insects while hiding, it will remove body odor, enable more successful hunting, and some even claim it will hide a human's scent from dogs.

Depending on your location, there are several different materials that make an excellent fuel for your fire. Dry pine needles, Spanish moss, dry hickory and other low flame, high smoke tender can be used. You may want to visit with some older gentlemen hunters in your area to see what they used back in the day before chemical retardants became available.

A final note on smoke bathing: smoke (from the fire) can be seen and smelled by humans from some distance away. If you are going to use this technique, you should do so at a time/place where detection by other two-legged mammals is not an issue. The actual smoke scent on your person will not give you away, but the fire might be a problem.

7.3.3 POISON PLANTS

Poison plants abound in most of the United States. According to www.WIKIPEDIA.com, poison ivy (***Toxicodendron radicans)*** and its cousin poison oak (***Toxicodendron diversilobum)*** can be found in over 80% of the United States. Most people get a nasty rash, which will eventually run its course with common household treatments. These cures may not exist in a TEOTWAWKI life.

Different people have various reactions to poison plants, so I would recommend you research what is common in your area of operation, and learn to identify it. If you are one of the lucky people who have no reaction to these plants, then their presence might indicate an effective hiding spot, although they normally do not grow in dense foliage.

One very serious word of advice when it comes to poison plants – **DO NOT** use these plants for any sort of fire. Inhaling the smoke from burning poison plants can be deadly, even with today's medical facilities.

EXERCISE

Most state and local parks provide free pamphlets that document poisonous plants in the area. Pick one up, and walk through the park identifying the various local species.

7.4 NOISE DISCIPLINE

Nothing will give away your position faster than making noise. In a wooded environment where visual distances are limited by foliage, hearing becomes the primary sensory input. Equipment rattling, coughing, sneezing, or any other noises can give you away. I avoid Velcro fasteners wherever possible because of the distinct noise they make.

There are a variety of noises that can ruin the perfect hiding place. Slapping at a biting insect is almost a sub-conscious reaction. That noise can be heard for long distances.

Charging a round into a rifle breach is a dead giveaway, with an emphasis on "dead."

In order to avoid noise issues, you need to think through almost every potential situation you may encounter while hiding. How are you going to eat? Drink?Take notes? All of these actions should be executed without making noise.

EXERCISE

Sit and make a list of everything you might have to perform while hiding. Do you have a wound that requires the dressing to be changed? Will you be there long enough to need a snack or meal? How are you going to take your canteen off of your belt silently?

Put on your gear and have a family member close their eyes. Perform one of the tasks and see if they can identify what you just did. If they can tell you what task you just performed, they win. If they can't, you win.

7.5 MOVEMENT DISCIPLINE

The human eye is very good at detecting movement. A good scout learns to stare unfocused at an area for long periods of time, waiting on movement. It requires strong discipline to stay absolutely stationary for extended periods of time. In reality, it is next to impossible to accomplish zero movement, but what you can learn to do is move so slowly it reduces the opportunity anyone will notice.

There are some movements that are next to impossible to control or predict.

How are you going to urinate?

What if an insect is biting you?

What if you have an itch?

EXERCISE

Try this test:

In any outside area, pick a spot where you will not look out of place. A lounge chair in the backyard, lying by the pool, or simply siting on your front porch will all work fine.

Take any inexpensive tape recorder and start recording. Sit the recorder on your lap.

Stay in the spot for 30 minutes with the tape recorder running.

After the time has expired, turn off the recorder and rewind the tape.

Listen to the recording. If you moved at all, the recorder will have picked up the movement, typically as a rustling sound.

How many times did you move?

Thirty minutes is not a long time. Some missions may require you remain stationary for hours. I once had a bet with a friend that he could not remain stationary even if watching a good football game on his favorite couch. The tape recorder revealed over 15 movements in two hours.

Controlling movement is truly a matter of discipline. Even the most highly trained snipers move. The difference is the speed and control of the movement. Snipers may crawl through an area at less than a foot per minute. They may have an itch, but will take five minutes to move a few inches to scratch. They think before they move, and you should learn to do the same.

Try the above exercise again, concentrating on moving slowly. You will find that the tape recorder does not detect slower movements. With any luck, an observer will miss the slower movement as well.

7.6 A GOOD SHOVEL

Quite frankly, digging sucks. There is nothing worse than working up a grime-encrusted sweat digging your spider hole, only to encounter a root the size of a New York City subway tunnel about halfway through. I once commented to a friend that I had become an expert in all things root bound.

Military entrenching tools are, in reality, short handled torture devices designed by sick minded, evil engineers who have never dug a hole to live in. They clearly believe guys who carry rifles relish blood blisters and have spines made of titanium.

There are a few non-military shovels available, but in reality, I have yet to find one that is much more effective. The problem is in the length of the handle. The shorter the handle, the less leverage you can apply to the soil. Less leverage equals more muscle power required.

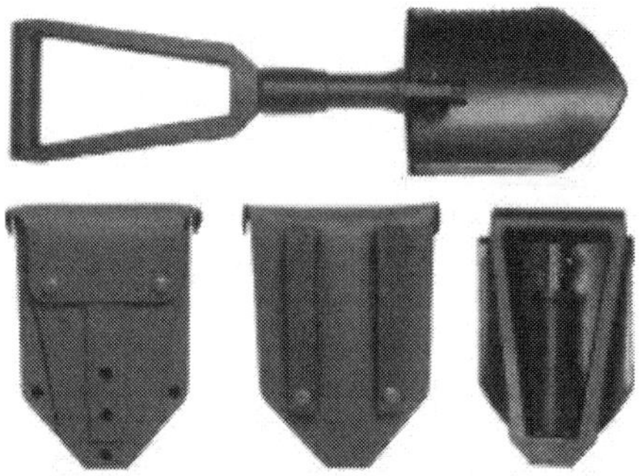

Longer handles are practically impossible to carry as an individual. The old Soviet Army issued their troops with a medium length handled shovel that I once tried out. The handle was great – but the quality of the steel in the spade was horrible. I went back to a good old Army surplus tri-fold E-Tool.

The proper method of using an entrenching tool is not the same as the shovel in your garage. With a long handled shovel, you would typically put your boot on the base of the spade, push down, and then toss the shovel full of dirt.

The E-Tool is supposed to be utilized more like a garden hoe. The spade locks into a 90-degree angle, which is then used to strike downward like a hoe. Once enough soil has been loosened, then the blade is locked into a normal position, and the tool acts like a short handled shovel. This often does not work as advertised, and you end up using it like a normal shovel anyway.

Why am I ranting about something as simple as a shovel? The reason is simple; sometimes the best positions to hide are below ground.

A modern day NATO E-Tool weighs about 1.5 pounds and is fairly robust. While the technology has reduced the weight, no one has yet to address sore backs from digging a hole using less than optimal leverage.

We preppers most likely won't have to worry about deep foxholes or fighting positions. What may save our lives is a good hide. For this reason, I suggest you invest in an E-Tool that provides the longest handle available. Some other suggestions:

- Keep the blade of the spade as sharp as possible. If the quality of the steel will allow it, your E-Tool should be as sharp as your knife.

- Never use the spade to cut thick roots. Use an axe or hatchet. What's worse than running into a root? Breaking your E-Tool while trying to cut through that root means finishing the hole by hand. Use something more robust to sever roots.

- Pick a low spot, natural trench, or drainage route to begin with. You will be surprised at how much digging it takes to make a good hole. The less you have to disturb earth, the better. If a deep enough rut is found, you might avoid any digging at all, but don't count on it. There is *never* a deep enough natural spot for a full sized human body and gear. At least I have never seen such a sight.

EXERCISE

You knew this was coming didn't you? Go dig a hole. Seriously, now, go try it. A word of caution, most public parks frown on people digging them up, so I would advise you to do this exercise on private land. If nothing else, you can tell the neighbors you are burying a pet if inquiries are made.

It is not the practice of digging the hole that is important. Anyone can do that. Doing this exercise fosters a realization of the time investment that must be dedicated to this task, as well as the opportunity to test your equipment. I am often surprised by the number of people who recoil at this suggestion. So many preppers plan on cultivating a garden and raising their own food. As soon as the gasoline runs out for the rototiller, you are going to be working a shovel to plant crops. You most likely are going to bury trash. Any time spent in the field means "cat holes" to bury human waste. I firmly believe my life in the post-TEOTWAWKI existence means I and mother earth are going to become fast friends. All of us will most likely become experts in excavation.

For the purposes of this book, you need to understand how long digging in general takes.

If you are being pursued and consider digging a spider hole to hide in, you had better be sure you have enough time.

If you schedule your scouting objective in order to arrive an hour before dark and dig your hide, you may be digging in the dark.

Record the time it takes, and use it as a rule of thumb for future activities.

One additional note – this is the most mundane, boring exercise in this book.

7.7 CAMOUFLAGE AND DISGUISE

Many people initially confuse camouflage with hiding. This is a mistake. You could wear the perfect ghillie suit and yet be easy to find if walking through the woods making noise. Camouflage is a component of hiding, like noise discipline, movement discipline, and position.

Military training uses an acronym when teaching the subject of camouflage – BLISS.

Blends in with surroundings
Low in silhouette
Irregular in shape
Small in size
Secluded

All of these items are based off of the capabilities of human observation as described above. While these are excellent guidelines to use initially, the typical survival situation may require camouflage techniques be taken to a more advanced level.

For example, the secluded item above may be completely impractical in a post-SHTF world. It is not unreasonable to prepare for camouflage in an urban area. Keep in mind that the military is training soldiers on how to get back to their units – not long-term survival in a hostile world.

Technically, there is a difference between camouflage and disguise. While the end goal may be the same, the difference is in not being *seen* versus not being *identified*.

Both camouflage and disguise require keen observation skills to be successful. One must be able to discern the detail of color, texture, and structure of the surrounding area. The secret of great camouflage is not to stand out – to blend in and not be noticed. The only way to accomplish this is to study the area where you intend to hide.

Disguise is addressed in the chapter on infiltration.

Most of the branches of the military provide what is named **S**urvival, **E**vasion, **R**esistance, and **E**scape (SERE) training. These programs provide invaluable skills to students who may be operating in hostile combat environments. The average prepper has a different set of potential problems if living in a post-collapse world. Military SERE training relies heavily on friendly, organized forces eventually being part of the solution to problem. Students are trained on how to evade hostile forces until they can reach, or be reached by friendlies. The average survival scenario doesn't have friendly, organized forces in play. You are completely on your own or at best have a small group of individuals with differing levels of training.

7.8 EXAMPLES - USING CAMOUFLAGE TO HIDE

We will cover camouflage in three separate sections – urban, woodland and desert. The concepts of good camouflage are the same, regardless of surrounding conditions. The **BLISS** rules, as described above, apply no matter what the conditions.

One of the most common methods of camouflage is the ghillie suit. If you have never prepared your own ghillie, there are some facts you need to know:

* It can take up to six hours to create a ghillie. The weaving of foliage, burlap, cotton, or plastic strips into the mesh of the suit takes a lot of time. Be patient.

* The type of material being used to create the ghillie is always a compromise. Natural vegetation, trimmed from local plants will always provide the best blending. It is also the most uncomfortable to wear and can be the heaviest. Strips of burlap or

cotton feel better against your body, but are heavy, especially if wet. They can also be very hot. Strips of plastic, if available, are both lightweight and comfortable. They, however, will make the most noise.

* Color is always the first consideration, followed closely by shape and then texture. If you have to compromise among the three when selecting material, sacrifice shape and texture before color.

* When setting up a hide, spider hole or other fixed camouflaged position, don't think you won't have to move around. Leave yourself room to shift body position, take a bathroom break, or eat. If you are taking the time to create a non-mobile hide, then you are planning to stay there for a while. Make it as comfortable as possible.

* In any terrain, the local soil is always your friend. If natural adhesives are combined with the local dirt, good color blending is easy. Tree sap, oil from crushed plants, and even the tissue from some animals makes an excellent bonding agent. If you don't have the right color ghillie materials, apply some natural glue and rub the strips around in the dirt. Good mud, clay, or damp soil works as well.

7.8.1 URBAN CAMOUFLAGE

City landscapes tend to be squared, or boxy as compared to woods or countryside. This can be a real challenge when considering camouflage. With a little creativity and imagination, one can find plenty of ways to hide in urban areas.

Military snipers are often considered the ultimate masters of hiding. Many of their methods were originally developed during WWII as the destructive battles, sieges and campaigns took place in the towns and cities of Europe. The sniper battles in such places as Stalingrad are legendary among the long-range shooters. Rubble and debris from bombed out infrastructure made excellent hiding spots and generally increased the effectiveness of sniping. The jungles of Vietnam added a second chapter to the sniper's handbook as this represented the first war where night vision was commonly used. Baghdad and other Iraqi cities added their own contributions to sniper lore, and some new techniques were even created in those conflicts. The current world's record for the longest documented kill took place in Afghanistan.

As discussed above, one of the most important aspects of hiding is choosing a position that will be avoided by people. Try and select a location that is naturally isolated from anyone that would be in the area.

It is impossible to predict the conditions of any urban landscape after a collapse of society. Many people are fascinated by movie images and written predictions of post-apocalyptic cities. These works of fiction have little basis in fact, and while entertaining, should not be used as a guideline for your preparations.

There are places in today's world where government has broken down completely, and the inhabitants have survived without organized rule for several years. A quick study of these areas can be enlightening and at minimum provide a more factual backdrop for your planning.

Currently, Somali is probably the closest reality of a TEOTWAWKI environment that can be studied today. For those of you who are not familiar with this little country (well, it was a country) on the horn of Africa, it has been the victim of years of civil war, brutal dictatorships and general anarchy since 1991.

Somali is probably best known to most Americans from the book and movie "Black Hawk Down" where 19 U.S. military personnel were killed in a single operation. The United Nations has been in Somali in one form or another since 1991.

There are many similarities between Somali and potential TEOTWAWKI situations here in the U.S.A. In fact, were it not for thousands of tons of food being shipped to the area by international relief agencies, it would probably be the perfect example. One has to assume that given TEOTWAWKI, no one will be shipping the United States any food.

The State Department report on Somali reads like a horror novel. It lists incidents of slavery, kidnapping, beheadings, piracy, rape, summary executions, suicide bombers, amputation as punishment, and so many other horrific acts I can't even list them all.

It also notes an expansive cast; encompassing organizations, governments, terrorist groups and clans so extensive that you can't follow the players. What is important to note for us preppers is that the deterioration of the Somali society has pitted all of these groups against each other.

In a TEOTWAWKI world, there is a strong chance our population will behave like the population of Somali. Our cities, when stressed, will probably respond similarly, if not the same.

As you study Somali, one inescapable fact is the number of refugees, or the enormity of the displaced population. We have all read the opinions of various "survival experts" who claim that people will not leave our cities given SHTF. They predict that rural preppers will be relativity safe from roaming gangs of city dwellers scouring the countryside looking for food and plunder. This has not been the case in Somali. The various factions fighting for power either follow or are embedded with the refugees. The refugees will do *anything* to escape the violence or find food, and thus wander around the country like nomads, trying to stay one step ahead of the next firefight.

A Danish study found that 74% of the Somali households had weapons. Only 50% of U.S. households own weapons. To me, this dispelled a popular myth that, "We Americans will be civil to each other because we are so well armed." Somalia boasts a higher percentage of weapon ownership, and clearly, there is nothing civil about their current situation.

It is very enlightening that most of the organized groups were either ethnic (clans) or religious in nature. I have often wondered if the underlying racial and ethnic tensions in our country would result in post-TEOTWAWKI groups being formed along those lines. What about our religions? Will the Baptists unify against the Mormons? I know this sounds a little silly, but open conflict between radical religious elements has happened in recent times – think about Northern Ireland.

The provisional government, backed by the United Nations, has holed up in a hilltop Alamo and has little to no control. Many preppers believe that federal, state, or local governments will maintain control of at least the cities. While I have to somewhat agree with that perception, Somali gives evidence otherwise. The largest city, Mogadishu, is by far the most violent area of the country – <u>and</u> the home of the government.

The United Nations Commission on Human Rights report on Somali estimates that in 1991, when the civil war broke out, there were over 400,000 deaths in one year. This equates to 5% of the estimated population at that time. If the same occurred here, we would suffer 16,000,000 dead. What I take from that "projection" is that there will be a lot of people left. This again displaces the thought that if TEOTWAWKI were to occur, there would <u>not</u> be many people left to fight over the remaining resources.

The situation in Mogadishu indicates people will remain in the cities, no matter how horrific they become. It is reasonable to assume portions of our population will react the same way.

EXERCISE

Use the internet, or other resources, to study areas where society has broken down. Somalia, Beirut, Serbia-Kosovo, Sudan, and even Northern Mexico can be subject matter for research. During Operation Iraqi Freedom, certain regions of Iraq were without any rule of law for short periods. Read the perspective of citizens living in those regions during these times. Learn how the population reacted in different environments. Base your plan on actual historical or current events. A good web search will provide reference information for Somali or any other area that has experienced a time without rule of law. Any public library should contain factual resources documenting what life is "really like" or how people actually coped. While this is not as entertaining as watching zombie movies on television, it will provide a more realistic mind set for your preparations.

Regardless of the reason, we may have to visit an urban area after TEOTWAWKI. We may be driven there for food, medical supplies or to rescue a family member. Perhaps we just need to pass through on our way elsewhere.

While the materials used to hide in a cityscape will differ from other terrain, the methods are the same as described above.

The picture above shows a common urban scene that could be practically any neighborhood in the U.S. There is a man hiding in this picture. He is in a comfortable spot from which he can observe, eat, drink and even fight if necessary.

The area shown in the photograph is less than 25 meters from a busy street. The man hiding in the picture was there for a considerable amount of time and was never detected by cars or pedestrians passing by. If not for weapon's safety, he could easily have kept his rifle pointed at the cameraman.

Our man is now standing to show his position. He was covered with a camouflaged netting and hiding in the pile of trash. The netting or ghillie "parka," is covered in plastic trash bags to help him blend in.

A picture of our scout, now uncovered.

While the black and white images don't provide a color perspective, it is safe to say this man wouldn't have been detected, even by someone walking right up beside him. Short of someone digging through the trash pile looking for food (or being picked up by the garbage truck), he could have stayed in the position for hours.

This particular black plastic ghillie suit took about 30 minutes to create and was surprisingly robust. To begin with, two large black plastic "lawn and leaf" bags were cut into flat sheets.

Our survival net was laid out flat on the floor, and safety pins were used to secure the sections of bag to the net.

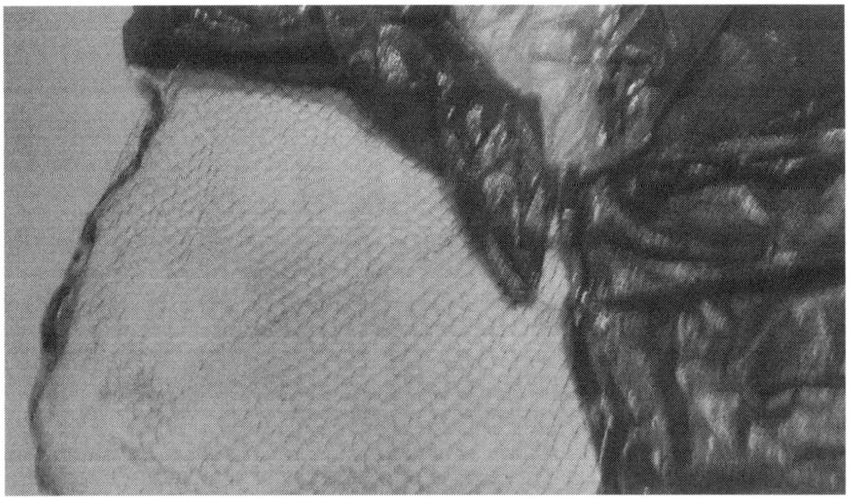

To add color, texture and stability, the ties from the trash bag were woven through the net here and there. Some old, crumpled papers were woven into the net to add texture.

The survival net's supports were used as "tent poles" to give the net a rounder, non-human shape.

Had it rained, our man would have remained relatively dry due to his makeshift plastic raincoat. While we made our camouflage in advance, in reality it could have been done in the field. If the scout had his survival net and some safety pins, he could have scavenged a few existing trash bags to complete his cover.

We could have just as easily attached cardboard boxes, industrial packaging, or even bubble wrap. Any waste material that would be common to the area could be used.

While we used safety pins in the example above, paper clips, small bits of wire or even rubber bands could have been applied. Unlike a dedicated ghillie suit, our man could disassemble his hide in a few minutes, store it in a MOLLE pouch and been able to move without hindrance.

7.8.2 WOODLAND CAMOUFLAGE

Most hunters know how to implement good cover in wooded areas. The amount of foliage, irregular shapes and shortened lines of visibility make this environment the easiest in which to conceal oneself.

The secret to effective woodland camo is texture and color. The most common varieties of ghillie suits are designed for wooded areas. There are some operational issues with "rag bags" in deep woods. It is easy to become snagged on thorns. Many types of materials become extremely heavy if they get wet, from either perspiration or rain. Speaking of perspiration, wearing burlap or other cloth ghillie during hot summer weather is hot...damned hot.

Most ghillie suits are not designed to be worn over equipment, such as load vests or packs. This defeats the purpose. In addition, some designs can hinder movement, like running.

One alternative is to use your survival net as a ghillie parka or veil. There is no shortage of materials that can be used for color or texture. One of my favorites is the plastic shopping bags common to almost every store. They come in all colors, are thin, extremely lightweight, waterproof and best of all – free!

It is easy to cut them up into strips and weave them into your netting. Afterwards, if available, give the plastic a shot of spray paint to meld into the local colors. Another coloring option would be to drag the net through loose leaves, mud, or pine needles. If it rains, they are waterproof and if applied thick enough, can even provide some level of protection as a parka.

While the black and white pictures below, required for printing, do not do justice to the camouflage, the effect is still clear.

The scout in the picture above is using his survival net with local foliage and leaves threaded into the net. He is exactly 20 steps away from the photographer. It took almost 40 minutes to cut and weave the materials into the net. This is an important consideration in any planning. If you don't have a lot of experience with camouflage in the field, you need to understand it takes a considerable amount of time to create a good hide.

The picture above shows the scout unveiled. He had been sitting comfortably resting against his pack. When signaled, he pulled off the net and stood.

Manmade camo material should be easy to acquire, even in a TEOTWAWKI life. Old shirts, plastic tablecloths, rags and many other materials can be cut and woven into a net or MOLLE ladders. Even paper can be used for short-term needs.

The picture below shows our scout using plastic shopping bags that have been cut and woven into a net. The scout is lying prone, with his weapon pointed at the photographer. This outfit took over 90 minutes to create. The picture was taken at 35 steps away.

We asked the scout to rise, take a knee, and be ready to engage (below).

Finally, the scout unveiled (below).

Any experienced hunter could purchase or create the same level of camouflage. Our examples are intended to communicate the importance of mobility, comfort and flexibility given evasion, infiltration or scavenging activities.

There are dozens of different methods to achieve the same results. What is important is given our premise, you have to be ready to run or fight given little notice. The stakes in a post-SHTF world will most likely be higher than any hunting trip or paintball match.

7.8.3 DESERT CAMOUFLAGE

Many professionals consider hiding in the desert to be the most difficult camouflage of all. The lack of vegetation, raw materials, and open lines of sight can be problematic. Arid areas also have positive attributes, such as being easier to dig than root infested woodlands. Other advantages are the lack of color differential in most dry landscapes and the prevalence of heavy rock formations, which disrupt the flatlands.

You will find that in relatively level areas, going sub-terrain is desirable. In addition to concealment, a shaded, covered hide will be cooler and more comfortable in most situations. In rocky deserts, shade is again important to consider for both temperature control and blending.

The interior pulp of many cacti or local hard scrub can be a great adhesive. This substance, combined with windblown sand and dust will eventually make almost anything blend into the surrounding color scheme.

7.8.4 RANDOM THOUGHTS ON HIDING

One of the major concerns while hiding is someone "busting your six," or sneaking up behind you. In an urban area, you may have to hold up in an abandoned home or building and these structures typically have more than one doorway. A trip wire might be affective, but inside of a building, they can be easily detected. One option is to use your survival net and some small hooks to hang your net over a door.

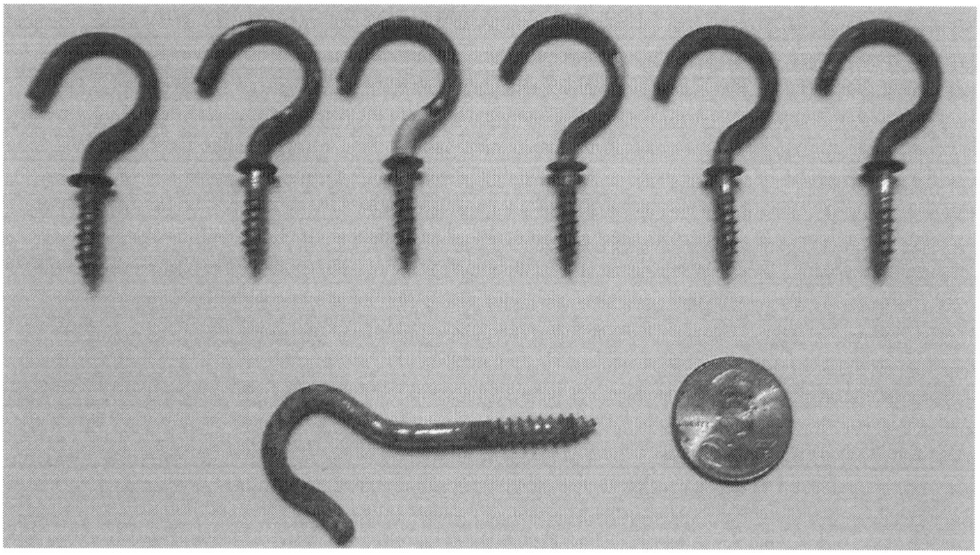

You simply mount the hooks into a stud (normally bordering the frame of the doorway), and hang the net tightly on the hooks, thus covering the door. Any sort of noisemaker can be hung in the net to provide additional warning. A small can with rocks or two pieces of metal that will "rattle" if the net is disturbed.

The purpose of the net and subsequent noise is to avoid being surprised. Nothing is worse than surprise in a fight.

This type of area denial system will slow down a breach. It will not stop a determined entry effort, but you will have some warning that someone is behind you or in another part of the structure.

This exact same method can be used to secure your bug out location, windows, or other entry-point weaknesses.

Another consideration for hiding is comfort. If you are going to be in any location for an extended period of time, you should select a position that allows for physical comfort. The emphasis of this book is focused on hiding in a post-collapse world. Stress levels will likely be high, and the consequences of mistakes deadly. Cramps, stiff joints, and tired muscles will degrade your capabilities, level of alertness, and general morale.

Using camouflage, ghillie suits, spider holes and other techniques often results in discomfort. The irritation involved with being poked by plant stems, itchy grass against skin, insects, and other factors involved in a good hiding spot are worth considering. Rain ponchos, packs, pouches, and other gear on your person can be used to help somewhat, but you should always keep in mind that you may have to leave, and perhaps do so quickly. Having your pouches disconnected, your poncho spread out, and your pack being used as a pillow can lead to abandoning your gear or causing a delay in any escape. The compromise will depend on the situation.

One mistake beginners make when it comes to camouflage is leaving a body part, limb, or weapon exposed. This is easy to do. One trick is to use your signal mirror and check your position. If you have a modern cell phone or other small digital movie camera, you can record yourself in the hide to determine if there are any "tells or tales."

Some people think that the branches of a tree are a good place to hide. Years ago, I learned a hard lesson about using a tree for any type of tactical activity. During my youth, hayrides were a common autumn activity. Since this activity took place around Halloween, pranks were a natural part of the festivities. One such hayride was organized by some of the more notorious bullies of the day and locale.

It didn't take much effort to find out who was driving the tractor, nor did it involve any intelligence coup to discover the route to be taken. A quick reconnaissance uncovered the perfect tree, complete with large branch overhanging the gravel path beneath. It was a great spot for a much deserved bushwhacking.

With military precision, a buddy and I visited a local farmer, claiming to need some pig manure for a school science project. A little water stirred in the mix before cooking in the sun for a few days, created a near perfect weapon of mass destruction.

On the eve of the event, my friend and I carried our well fermented bags of pig potpourri up that big tree. We waited for the tractor to head our direction, and before long we could see the headlights in the distance. The bags were strategically positioned. As the wagon passed underneath us, our pocket knives made quick slits in the plastic, and the fun began.

The bedlam in that hay wagon was something to see. Following the initial shock and awe, the sound of cursing and screaming made it clear we had hit our mark. We found this hilarious and had to take care not to fall from the tree while laughing.

All of a sudden, the tractor stopped.

This was not part of the plan! Why did the tractor stop? This was not good.

At first, a few of the enemy tried to climb the tree, but facing my boot as it thrust down at their heads discouraged that tactic. However, this only seemed to incite and motivate them more. It seems some people have zero sense of humor about these things. My buddy, thinking we could withstand the siege from our lofty position, proceeded to chide the onlookers with numerous comments about not noticing anything different about their odor. I, on the other hand, remember thinking they *actually* wanted to kill us. It was about then that some perceptive fellow figured out they were all standing on a gravel road, and thus had an unlimited supply of projectiles.

Now I don't know about you city folks, but the average country boy spends a significant portion of his early life throwing rocks. Some even develop significant skills. Our opponents were no exception, and it felt like some of them might need to consider pitching in the big leagues.

I hope all of the readers understand why I don't recommend hiding in trees.

7.9 HIDING CHECKLISTS AND TIMELINES

Creating empirical data on hiding can be difficult. No two hides are the same. I have taken six hours to create a good ghillie suit while in the field. During the spring, with lots of green foliage, the same exact task can take 30-40 minutes.

EXERCISE

Just like setting up a bivouac or fixing a meal, we need some level of DOPE on hiding. The only way to achieve this is to actually go into the field and collect it.

This can be problematic if you live in an urban area, but the need is still the same. If you wait until it everything falls apart, it may be too dangerous to go practice.

Rural areas are friendlier to this type of activity. Hunters typically use ghillie suits or hides for various types of game, so you wouldn't stand out or be noticed.

Everyone should experience the sheer joy of digging a spider hole on a hot day.

You should time yourself on all of these activities.

As you practice creating various types of hides, keep a chart like the one below.

Task	Total Time	Equipment Used
Ghillie on Net Spring Foliage		
Time to build Hide	1 hours	Knife Net Machete Fasteners
Time to take down Hide	.5 hours	Knife
Ghillie on Net Fall Foliage		
Time to build Hide	4 hours	Knife Net Machete Fasteners
Time to take down Hide	.5 hours	Knife
Spider Hole		
Time to build Hide	3 hours	Shovel Net Poncho
Time to take down Hide	.5 hours	

In later sections, the information above will be combined with previous exercises into a fully operational plan.

The time to create a good hide, **hide construction**, is often overlooked when it comes to the scheduling (timetable) of any given operation. There is nothing more frustrating than arriving at a hide site after dark, bumbling around in the bush trying to construct the hide, and then wondering all night how much of your body is exposed.

Overnight operations add even more complexity and can require more kit. Not only do you have to be concerned about creating a good hide, but now it must serve as camp and allow sleeping, eating, and other long-term activities.

8. HOW TO EVADE

Evasion is a critical skill for warfighters, snipers, and Special Forces operators. The ability to avoid others is utilized on practically every operation. For people who are preparing for a SHTF or TEOTWAWKI existence, evasion will likely play a different role in day-to-day activities. A soldier may be trying to avoid organized enemy sentries or patrols, while a prepper is up against less organized groups or random individuals.

Regardless of the ultimate reason to evade, the knowledge required to succeed is basically the same. There are three high level categories of evasion:

1. Evade on insertion or approach
2. Evade on egress or extraction
3. Evade pursuit

Each of the above three categories can be further divided into "hot" or "dirty" versus "clean" or "cold" evasion. Hot/dirty evasion is basically when shooting or fighting is involved. Clean/cold is when stealth is achieved - thus the phrase "clean getaway."

If you are approaching (insertion) a target, a cold situation is almost always desired. Hot approaches quickly become offensive operations, and that is a completely different category of skills and methods. For our purposes as preppers, if an approach turns dirty, then chances are the objective is over. We will most likely have to egress (run like hell) and try again another day.

The same can be said of an extraction that becomes hot – it most likely will turn into a full-fledged fighting retreat. In most cases, having an egress turn hot is undesirable, to say the least.

Avoiding pursuit is another matter altogether. Most people make the mistake of believing that evading pursuit is a simple concept of time and distance. You increase the distance between you and those who are hunting you. If practical, this can be a valid strategy, but there are often better alternatives than trying to outrun pursuit. Many people believe that they can move as fast as those chasing them and never be caught. If both parties start out even, with identical capabilities, this belief may prove true. This line of thinking is unrealistic however. In the field under stressful conditions, you have no way of knowing what the capabilities of the pursuers are. Do they have motorized vehicles, like ATVs? Are they using horses? Have they radioed ahead to a friendly party?

Evasion doesn't always involve avoiding discovery or being caught. If you allow someone to track you back to your original location, you have not executed a proper evasion. Even though you were never personally discovered or caught, the bad outcome is the same or perhaps even worse. While tracking is a difficult skill that has been overstated by years of Hollywood movies, there are those who are proficient in it.

8.1 SPECIAL EQUIPMENT

More than any other skill covered in this book, evasion requires proper load-bearing equipment and depends on a high level of competence using it. Evading an opponent can be physically demanding and require extended periods of rapid movement. If your gear doesn't fit properly or causes extra discomfort, this can lead to exhaustion. You also need a high level of confidence while on the run. Pouches that are constantly falling off or becoming entangled in other equipment are a distraction, and mental alertness will decline.

8.2 STALKING

Most preppers would use the term move or travel, but when it comes to evasion, stalking is perhaps a better description. Stalking through various terrains takes practice. Here are some common recommendations that should make any movement less noticeable:

- When walking upright, take half steps and do so slowly.

- With each step forward, place your weight on the forward foot using one of these methods:

(a) Outside ball of the foot first and then roll your weight inside until level on the ball of your foot. Keep feeling for branches that may crack under your weight. Since you are taking half steps, it should be easy to reposition your foot.

(b) Toe to heel, checking for branches as the weight comes down.

(c) Heel to toe, checking for branches as the weight comes down.

- If crawling is required, try to maintain as much distance between your hand falls and knee falls as possible. This will keep your silhouette lower and force you to keep a slow pace.

- If prone, do pushups to move yourself forward a bit at a time rather than dragging your body along the ground. Progress will be slow, but if you are prone, there is probably a reason not to move quickly anyway.

Walking, crawling or dragging without excessive noise or footprint is not difficult. It is recommended, however, that you practice with your full load on. The weight of rifle, pack and other equipment can cause balance issues and may restrict movement.

EXERCISE

Equipped as a normal hiker, visit a State or National Park with a full pack and gear. Find a remote area and practice walking without noise or footprint. If you have a companion along, try to track each other. Make a contest out of counting the number of indicators left by the other's passage. You should do this in as many different terrains as are available. Open field, dense woods, light woods, etc.

If you are alone, take a tape recorder along. Once in position, turn on the recorder and attempt to walk without noise. Replay the tape to see how you did. Many cell phones have recording capabilities if you don't own a dedicated tape recorder.

 **EXERCISE**

With the exercise above, time your travel. This is critical **DOPE** to know. How can you plan any operation without knowing your speed cross country, carrying a full kit?

This information will be used in later exercises.

If at all possible, you need the same information for traveling at night. Even with good quality night vision devices, you will move slower at night.

8.3 EVADE ON INSERTION OR APPROACH

Imagine the scenario of a warehouse in a post-collapse world. You believe the warehouse contains food and medical supplies, but have to pass through a populated area in order to scout it. Your route to an observation point is the **insertion** or **approach**. After finishing the reconnaissance, your path out is the **egress** or **extraction**.

There are a few very important guidelines that apply to both insertion and extraction:

(1) Travel at night whenever possible.

(2) Avoid ridges or high places where your silhouette can be easily seen.

(3) Always select a route with good cover as compared to a shorter distance. Take the longer route if it provides better concealment.

(4) Beware of fatal funnels, or natural geographical barriers that force travel through a narrow or limited passage. A bridge over a gorge is an excellent example. If you are discovered, the opponents will not have to give chase, they can simply close the bridge behind you.

(5) Avoid crossing highways, long flat roads, or rail lines if at all possible. If you must cross such an obstacle, do so at dusk or at night. If you must cross during the day, find a drainage pipe or other hidden place for safer passage.

(6) Know your next move before you make it. Look ahead some distance and plan on where you are going to stop next. Make sure there is cover. Choose an alternative in case you have to divert from the next spot at the last minute.

(7) Move at a speed that won't attract attention. If you are in a ghillie suit and crawling across an open grassy field, advancing at less than a foot per minute might be required. If you are disguised as a homeless person, walk slowly with your head down. Whatever the method of movement, don't rush or draw attention to yourself.

(8) Scan 360 degrees often. Once you arrive at a spot, scan your complete perimeter slowly. Make sure you are not being followed. Make sure no one took note of your arrival. Make sure opponents are not closing off your egress or extraction route.

For preppers, I would like to add another guideline:

(9) Always look for an uncommon or atypical route. Can you evade by staying on rooftops without silhouetting? Using sewers? Can you float down a waterway? Don't think in a purely two-dimensional way. Add height/depth to your thinking. Can you have a shorter insertion route by scouting from a higher place and observing from a greater distance?

8.4 EVADE ON EXTRACTION OR EGRESS

Once you have accomplished your task or goal, you have to leave the area. While the same guidelines apply to egress as to insertion, there are differences. If you have been on a raid for supplies, you may be heavier than before. Bulky loot can make noise or slow you down.

Another difference between insertion and extraction is that you may have left evidence of your presence. Leaving any sign of a visitor should be avoided. If you ate an energy bar, put the wrapper in your dump pouch. If you had to defecate, make sure you bury it well. In some cases, leaving behind signs of your visit is unavoidable. If your mission were to scavenge, you may have had to bust a door or break through a window. Cut fences, broken glass, and other physical evidence may indicate an intruder's presence and lead to pursuit.

8.5 EVADE PURSUIT

Being hunted is not a desirable experience. Unfortunately, it may be commonplace in a TEOTWAWKI life. There are two general methods to avoid capture:

- Outrun (outpace) the pursuit
- Make the pursuit pass you by, often called a "bypass"

If you are being chased by a group of men who have ill intent, the first action that comes to mind is to outrun them. Our brains are programmed to equate distance with safety. While this can be a valid method, you should not overlook bypass as an alternative.

There are many factors involved in deciding which method to attempt. It can be a very difficult choice. Not only are there several variables to consider, this analysis is normally taking place under very high stress levels.

8.5.1 OUTPACE

Being able to outrun pursuit is a combination of speed and direction. The hunters can be following your every footstep, but if you are faster, they will eventually lose the trail or give up. In reverse, if the hunters are faster but going the wrong direction, they will never catch you.

A key to successfully outrunning pursuit is sometimes referred to as "avoiding the 9s," which means never stay on any constant 90-degree course. The diagram that follows shows the improper route.

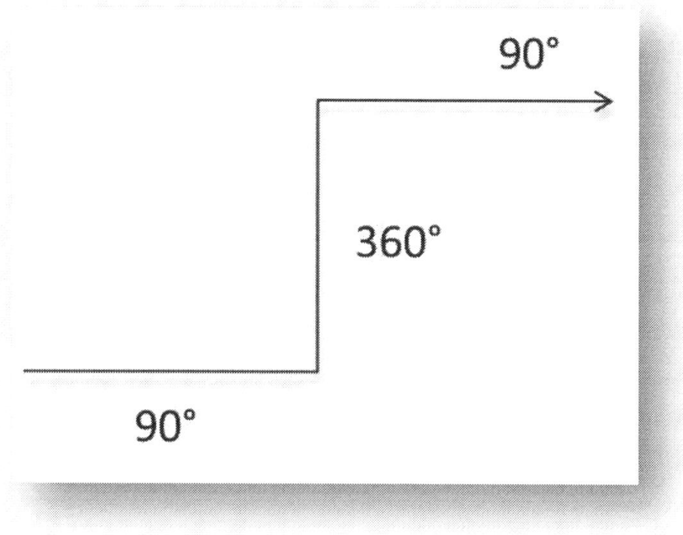

While it would seem like common sense to avoid running at right angles or in a straight line, many people will do exactly that. A shorter route that still avoids traveling in a straight line (still a 90) is shown below.

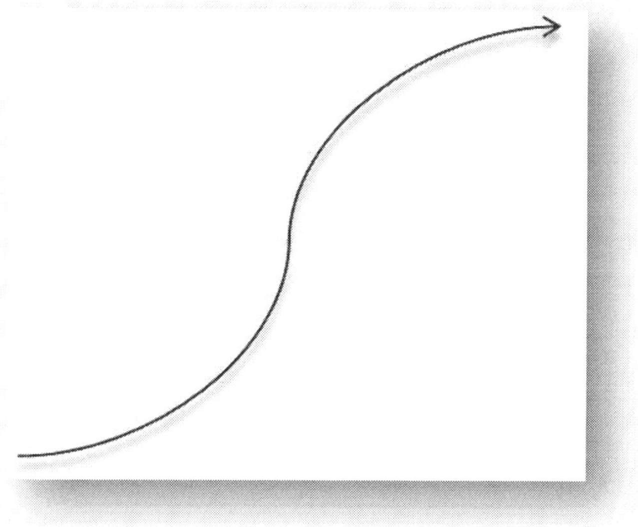

If you have ever watched a football game where the ball carrier is running in open field, he will avoid the 9s if he senses the pursuit is faster than he is. He will angle away toward the end zone rather than run straight up the field.

Another concern with outrunning an advisory is speed versus noise. It is difficult to move quickly without making sound in many terrains. The sound you generate can keep the hunters right on your trail and provide incentive for them to keep up the chase or increase their pace. Slowing down to avoid noise obviously allows for the bad guys to gain ground. Most military survival instructors teach their students to maintain a steady, moderate pace and avoid noise wherever possible. Avoid sprinting as well as creeping too slowly. Another important aspect of the speed versus noise dilemma is that your pursuers will make as much noise as you do while traveling the same speed. The more individuals they have, the more this effect is multiplied. A large group of men thrashing through the woods will generate enough racket to mask your noise.

One method to gain some distance on any pursuing force is to set a booby trap. Realistically, it doesn't even have to work. If discovered by the hunters, it will slow them down, and that means you can gain ground. Just about any device that appears lethal will work. Some fishing line, a shotgun shell, and a nail can be made to look like a good trap. Learning to set an effective, functional trap quickly is even better.

The probability of trained dogs being used in a TEOTWAWKI scenario is low, but still a possibility. Many people believe dogs are the ultimate pursuit technology, but this is inaccurate. Bloodhounds (and other trained canines) have several weaknesses or shortcomings that can be exploited by the savvy prey.

- Dogs are easily distracted by other animals like rabbits. Handlers have to keep their dogs constantly focused.

- Scent loses its potency quickly. Every minute that goes by makes it more difficult for dogs to maintain the trail.

- Dogs tire easily. They cannot keep up a rapid pace for nearly as many miles as a fit human. They require water breaks and are unable to drink on the run.

While there is no foolproof way to shake a good bloodhound, you can do several things to minimize their effectiveness. If you take the proper actions, you can actually make the dogs slow down the pursuit.

Pepper spray will not shake a dog off of a trail, but the animal will hesitate after encountering it. One method is to walk in small, tight circles, increasing the diameter each lap. When the circle is about 15 feet in diameter, spray a concentrated blast of pepper spray on the ground or low on a tree truck. Continue directly away from the spot.

Another method is to partially climb a tree now and then. The dogs will detect the scent going up the tree and stand barking and looking up. The handlers will have to verify you are not hiding in the tree and that takes time.

Despite what you see on television shows, water crossings are not effective against dogs unless the body of water is very wide. Your willingness to cross water may buy you some time if the hunters don't want to get wet, but the dogs will simply patrol the opposite bank until they pick up your exit point.

WARNING – Do not attempt a bypass evasion if dogs are being used.

The effectiveness of any pursuit, regardless of canines, is directly related to the skills of the hunters.

8.5.2 BYPASS

Utilizing bypass as a successful strategy is dependent on several factors concerning the pursuit, terrain, and equipment in your possession.

The most important consideration before implementing a bypass is how much time separates you and your tracker. If you don't have the time to prepare a proper hide, then bypass should not be attempted. How much time is required depends on your specific situation. Consider the following scenarios:

(1) You are being chased by several men through a wooded area. You believe they are 10 minutes behind. You are already wearing an affective ghillie suit that blends well with the surrounding foliage. There has been no indication they have dogs.

In the above scenario, executing a bypass is almost a no-brainer. You move at a good pace until finding the right spot and then rely on your camouflage. The hunters will probably pass right by you. Give them a little time, verify there is no follow-on, and then head the opposite direction.

(2) You are being pursued by several men through a wooded area. You believe they are only a few minutes behind. You don't have any camouflage on.

In this situation, the bypass is not a good idea. It will take you some time to create a good hide. Cutting branches or digging a spider hole under a fallen log eats away at your precious lead over the pursuit. You are better off to try and gain some distance (outrun) and then create your hide.

While it might be entertaining to play out several what-if scenarios, the two examples above describe the primary decision process clearly. You must have enough time (head start) to prepare a bypass hide. One of the most effective methods is to go underground - literally. A small, natural indentation in the forest floor can be turned into a hiding place if you have enough time to gather dead branches, leaves and other debris to cover yourself completely.

In a bypass situation, it is wise to be ready to fight. There is always the chance that a hunter will walk right up on you, regardless of how well you have hidden.

The odds of being detected when trying to implement a bypass evasion are directly proportional to the number of pursuers. The pattern or formation of the hunters is also an important consideration.

A large formation of men will almost always form a skirmish line and sweep through an area. The larger the number of men in the formation, the smaller any gap between them will be. An example of a skirmish line follows.

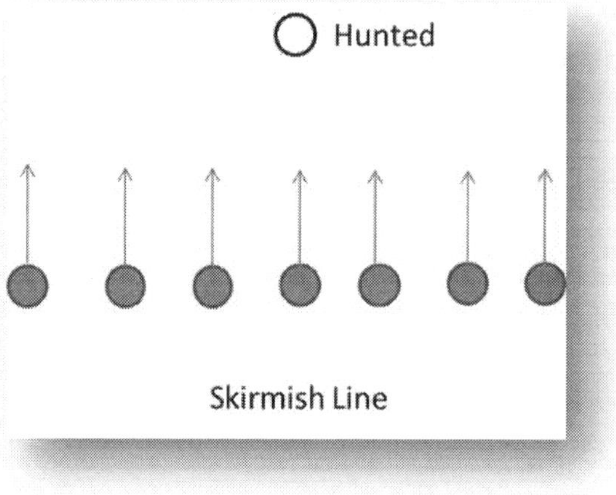

There are dozens of formations that are commonly used to search an area. All have various strengths and weaknesses. If you are trying to evade using a bypass, there is one specific category of search formation that you should be aware of – the follow-on. It is designed to snare someone using the bypass and can be very effective.

The follow-on splits the hunters into two groups, one conducting the initial search while the second lags behind waiting to catch anyone who slides through the initial group. The follow-on group will typically be a smaller number of people. A diagram showing the typical follow-on formation is shown below:

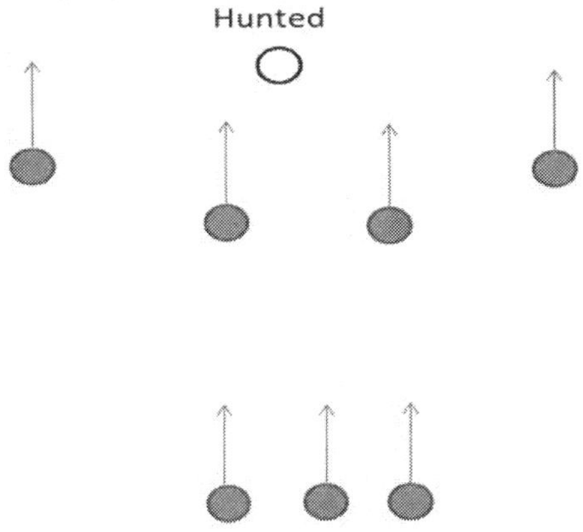

Follow-on Formation

The best method of defeating a follow-on formation is to be patient. After watching the initial group of hunters pass by, it is difficult to remain in the hide and wait. Human nature prompts us to immediately put distance between the threat and ourselves.

8.5.3 OFFENSIVE EVASION

In addition to bypass and outpace, there is another method – offensive evasion. It involves picking off the hunters one-by-one during the pursuit. I strongly recommend you avoid even thinking about using offensive evasion as a prepper. While several

Hollywood movies depict this as a valid, even heroic option, in reality it is a bad idea. The first issue with going on the offensive is that it is very difficult to kill a man without noise. Most people underestimate the mental impact of taking a human life up close and personal and do not have the training or experience to execute this type of action *silently*. Many professionals refer to this as "wet work," and it was given that name for a reason. A Special Forces operator with years of field experience might, just maybe, go on the offensive if being pursued by a small number of bumbling idiots. Unless you have similar skills, going aggressive is not a good idea.

It's just not worth the risk. In a TEOTWAWKI life, avoiding injury is going to be a top priority. Going offensive increases the odds you will be hurt badly. If the hunters are vulnerable to offensive actions due to their number or competence, then they are probably easy enough to lose anyway. If you start picking off their friends, they will probably not become frightened and leave. Their reaction will be to become angry, motivated, and even more alert. If eventually captured, the treatment received by the prisoner will no doubt reflect that anger.

EXERCISE

In terrain similar to your bug out location, take a walking trip from point A to point B. The distance should be at least a mile or so. While you are walking, take a notepad and paper along. At least ten times during the trip, find a good hiding spot. It should be somewhere to "hole up" if being chased. Note any special tools, camouflage, or other items that would make the spot perfect.

Take detailed notes and perform this exercise several times. Compile a list and look for similarities. For example, if in an urban area, are there large public trashcans every so often? What would it take to get inside of one? Manhole covers, sewers, building fire escapes, and other less traveled areas in which to hide should be noted.

In a rural area, are there drainpipes under the road, or fence lines with high weeds?

After a few trips, you should begin to notice commonly available hiding spots that can be used to evade pursuit.

You should also note open areas to be avoided. Long, flat roadways or railroad tracts, open fields and parks with sports fields should be avoided because of visibility issues.

9. HOW TO INFILTRATE

Even if narrowed to a military context, infiltration is a word with numerous meanings. For the average prepper operating in a post-TEOTWAWKI life, the best dictionary definition is "a clandestine action with subversive intent."

In strictly infantry terms, infiltration means to *bypass the enemy strongpoints in order to cause havoc in their rear areas*. General Oskar von Hutier is often credited with developing the tactic, but I personally believe raiders and guerrilla fighters have used these methods since the dawn of conflict, which probably coincides with the dawn of humanity.

There are many potential situations where the knowledge of basic infiltration skills may be useful in a post-collapse society. Consider the need to pass through a populated area that is too large to circumvent. You may find yourself in a life or death situation, in need of food, medicine or other critical items. Another possibility would be to rescue someone who has been captured, perhaps held for ransom. Obviously, no one can be 100% certain what level of government control will still exist in any given scenario. Nor can anyone predict how the surviving population will organize or band together. Infiltration may entail simply blending in, so as to pass through an area without being noticed. It could possibly mean breaching a government run food bank or penetration of a military camp. There is simply no way to know.

9.1 SPECIAL EQUIPMENT

- Optics (high powered riflescope or good binoculars)
- Pen and paper (preferable waterproof or watertight)
- Fishing line and weight (to detect trip wires)
- Materials for disguise (if applicable)

9.2 PLAN

Despite the unknowns of the future, there is a basic process for the planning of a complex operation, such as an infiltration.

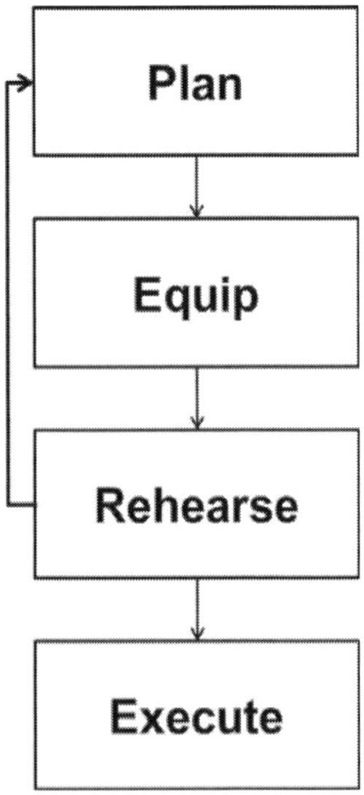

The key is a good plan. Like any dangerous, complex action, the simpler the plan, the more likely it is to succeed. In the words of General George S. Patton, "*Successful generals make plans to fit circumstances, but do not try to create circumstances to fit plans.*"

In addition, one should not confuse a simple plan with a bold one. Boldness is often unexpected or unprepared for by the opposing force. An example would be the attacks against America on 9-11. The shock generated by the audacity of the terrorist attack was, in some respects, more effective than the actual physical damage resulting from the attacks. Common questions in military and law enforcement communities at the time included, "How can we protect against someone who is willing to commit suicide? How do we secure our country against such a sophisticated, bold attack by people willing to sacrifice their lives for a cause?"

It is practically impossible to formulate any plan without some level of knowledge about the target, enemy, or area. In many cases, gathering intelligence (knowledge) is a plan unto itself. Don't fall into the trap of trying to create a plan with multiple contingencies based on a lack of knowledge. An example would be:

If there are no sentries, then

I will kick in the door and load up the food

but

If there is only one sentry, then

I'll disable him, and kick in the door and load up the food

but

If there is more than one sentry, then

I will cause a diversion, draw them off, kick in the door, and load food

or

....

A better plan would be:

Scout the target and determine the number of sentries.
Return home and formulate the second phase of the plan.

Performing a complete, detailed reconnaissance of any location to be infiltrated is critical. Regardless of the overall goal of the mission, some facts are required in all circumstances. It doesn't matter if the goal is to rescue a family member or scavenge food; there are basic deliverables of any reconnaissance that you will require later. What should be identified is:

> Details of the security, both human and non-human (dogs, fences, walls, etc.) of the target

> Details of the number of hostile defenders, what equipment they are carrying, and what their patterns are

- Do they have flashlights?

- Do they all take a drink from a common spot, or do they carry individual water?

- How much ammo do they carry?

> Drawings and notes of potential infiltration routes, egress routes and alternatives

> A detailed analysis of how "friendlies" enter and leave the target area. This may indicate booby traps or other area denial devices

> Are motorized vehicles available to the hostile group? Horses?

> Maps (hand drawn) of all structures, buildings, roads, paths, and sentries. Make sure to observe, noting all windows and lights, such as floodlights or spotlights

The deliverables generated by the planning phase should include:

> A clear, detailed objective of the mission

> A timeline of the mission

> The route in (insertion)

- Where are you going to eat

- Where are you going to sleep, or wait for dusk

> The route out (egress)

> Alternatives for both insertion and egress

> Rally point (if more than one person is involved)

> Methods to bypass the target's security

> Methods to retrieve, carry out loot, or accomplish the goal

Your plan should also include contingencies, such as weather. Can you execute the plan in a thunderstorm? Blizzard? High winds?

9.3 EQUIP

Preparing the equipment to be used during the infiltration is a simple sub-process if the plan is detailed enough and you have created the checklists recommended in previous sections. Each step of the plan should be checked to verify all necessary equipment is packed.

This should include the egress as well. If you are performing the infiltration to loot food, for example, you need some method to carry the food back. If you are going to rescue a family member, plan for their being injured or too weak to walk out with you.

You should also determine certain "it all went to hell" equipment. If you are discovered, will you have to shoot your way out? How many magazines should you bring? If you are chased and have to circumvent pursuit, do you have enough food packed for a longer route home?

9.4 REHEARSE

Rehearsal is where our equipment, skills, timeline, and plan are verified as a complete operation. As you have gone through the above sections, you have collected an equipment list, empirical data on time allocation, and developed a specific set of actions to be executed. Now it is time to put them all together and verify the strategy works.

The most important part of the plan is to rehearse every single step. Before a Special Forces team executes a complex operation, they know every detail so they can "sleepwalk" through the mission. In some cases, it has been reported that entire structures have been replicated at secret locations to be used for rehearsals. One of these rumors involved Colonel Charles Beckwith ordering a model of the U.S. Embassy in Tehran, Iran to be constructed so that Group Delta operators could rehearse for Operation Eagle Claw, the failed Iranian hostage rescue mission in 1980.

The above-mentioned failure in the Iranian desert was due to a change in the desert floor being used as an airstrip. It had been surveyed only a few weeks before and found to have hard-packed sand. When the aircraft began to arrive during the mission, three inches of sandy powder had accumulated which led to engine failure and crashes. Expect changes to the information you have gathered. Your plan should allow as many contingencies as possible.

While it may not be practical to build a scale model of the target, details and rehearsals are constantly executed and evaluated by professional infiltrators. We preppers should do the same whenever possible. Practicing in as many different environments as possible will help identify different opportunities in a real life situation.

EXERCISE

Here are the steps I recommend for minimal rehearsal:

(1) Load up all of your gear. Everything should be as it will be during the actual infiltration. Magazines full, water full, pack, kit, vest – everything as if you were going for real.

(2) Using the exact same mode of transportation, (walking, driving, etc.), go a reasonable distance away from home (or whatever the location). The practice location should be somewhere private.

(3) Take a printed copy of your plan and walk through every single step:

- If you are going to be spending the night in the field, set everything up.

- If the plan requires a meal, make one.

- If you will be observing from a tree or roofline, climb something similar.

- If the goal is to escape with some loot, fill your looter's bag with something heavy, and walk some distance with it and your gear.

(4) As you execute the steps of your plan, you will probably encounter unanticipated needs or issues, such as missing gear or limitations. Make note of these and modify the plan and your equipment.

(5) Repeat as necessary.

Always remember – failure will often occur due to details that seem minor or unimportant in the planning stage. The secret to success is to revise the plan.

It is impossible to have a good plan without practice and rehearsal. Don't think you can just mentally walk through a complex mission and plan it out. Take your time and fill in the details. Physically execute every step, even if it is as mundane as taking a drink of water from your canteen. If your goal is looting, make sure to approximate the weight of the loot and duplicate that weight as closely as possible when you add rocks in your looter's bag and walk around with it.

9.5 EXECUTE

When it's time to actually execute the plan, it is normal to experience emotions ranging from apprehension to outright fear. If you have rehearsed and practiced enough, this will fade as the mission begins. Hopefully, adrenaline will compensate for any natural anxiety. Most experienced professionals will tell you that the guy who is not afraid is overly confident, and thus dangerous.

Previous chapters covered hiding and evasion. The capabilities described in those chapters will normally be used during an infiltration. While you are traveling to and from any target, you may have to utilize those skills to hide from sentries and evade patrols. The need to understand how to hide and evade if discovered and thus pursued is obvious.

9.5.1 USE THE NIGHT

As covered in the equipment sections of this book, night vision is one of the most valuable tools available to the survivalist. Its uses for infiltration are infinite. Beyond the obvious task of avoiding hostiles because you can see them and they can't see you, there are some lesser-known advantages to night vision.

One of my personal favorites is driving at night without headlights. If you have a motorized vehicle at your disposal, you can remove the fuses for headlights, brake lights, and dome lights. A high quality generation III NVD will actually provide better visibility while driving than normal headlights.

You can move quickly through wooded terrain using night vision, even if the device is not head mounted or goggles. Using a NVD monocle, the proper method is to look through the device and chart your footfalls for 20 steps or so, commit that to memory and then stop after that number of steps. You repeat the process until you reach your destination.

A note about using the night:

Don't assume you are the only one who can see at night. Soldiers have been fighting without NVDs at night for thousands of years. Non-enhanced human eyes can see well at night, especially with a good moon or bright star field.

A flashlight with a red filter is essential equipment for night operations. White light (emitted by a normal flashlight) degrades your natural ability to see at night and can be seen for longer distances than red light. There are several models available from both military surplus and commercial sources. I recommend a light that has the different colored lenses built in, rather than as an attachment. I always end up losing the attachments.

EXERCISE

With night vision or a flashlight, practice walking by charting your steps. Illuminate your path for a few moments and commit your next 15-20 steps to memory and then execute. Warning – in a wooded area, wear safety glasses until you become proficient, as a sharp stick in eye can ruin the fun.

9.6 DISGUISES

While camouflage was addressed extensively in ***How to Hide***, the use of disguise is normally associated with infiltrations. Disguises and camouflage share many of the same principles, but also differ in several aspects.

In order to clarify some of the unique facets of affective disguises, the scenario described in the introduction of this book can be used as an example. In that section, I claimed that I could walk through any major metropolitan area undisturbed. Furthermore, I bragged this could be accomplished while carrying the gear required for a full assault – equipment that would normally draw the attention of the local authorities, if not the SWAT team.

In reality, this would be very simple to do. I would merely disguise myself as a homeless person, pulling my possessions along in a ragtag suitcase. I have actually performed this action. Creating this disguise was easy and inexpensive:

- I went to a second hand store and purchased some clothing that was a few sizes too large. Dull, mismatched colors and patterns were the key selection criteria.

- The clothing was dumped in the parking lot (at night) and run over with my truck a few times. A small mud puddle helped with the effect.

- I then tied the clothes onto the trailer hitch of the truck, and dragged the clothes up and down our street a few times.

- The suitcase was found at a garage sale and had seen better days. I applied some duct tape in key areas and dragged it through some mud.

- I bungee corded another old shirt and some newspaper in a plastic trash bag to the handle.

- My regular baklava mask (with some dirt applied) and a pair of old cotton gardening gloves with the fingers cut off rounded out the clothing part of my disguise.

- My worn boots, one tied, and one untied with the tongue flapped forward, rounded out my hobo look.

- I rubbed some dirt on my face and hands, but not too much. Spray on tanning products would work as well if you were a light skinned or pale person.

The suitcase contains my 1st line equipment, including my M4 Carbine, broken down into two pieces (as described in the weapons chapter above).

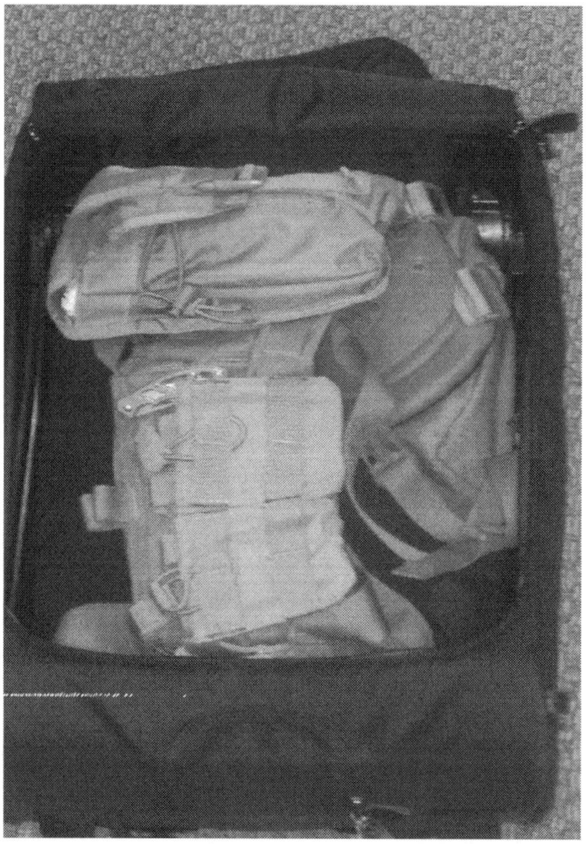

Unfortunately, every major American city has some population of those who are down on their luck or choose to live the hobo life. Most citizens avoid these folks for several reasons. Mental health issues are common, and many of our nation's homeless raise pocket cash by begging. Physical health issues, such as lice, body odor, and respiratory diseases are also known to exist in this segment of the population.

In our example, I walked around shuffling my feet with my head bent low. If anyone had come near, I would have started talking to myself or mumbling.

Upon arrival at the ultimate destination, I can switch from down-on-my luck Charlie to a more useful mode (*magazines removed)* in a few minutes.

When you consider the properties of camouflage, disguising oneself as a homeless person fulfills all of the requirements. My disguise adhered to the military acronym of **BLISS** in that it:

Blends in with surroundings – Homeless people are common.
Low in silhouette – I am perceived as unthreatening as long as I don't transverse wealthier neighborhoods.
Irregular in Shape – There is no outward evidence I am heavily armed.

Small in size – A bent posture and sullying walk make me appear harmless and not menacing.
Secluded – People will not want to approach me. I am worthless to predators.

As long as I keep up the façade, the disguise meets the requirements of **noise** and **movement** discipline as well.

EXERCISE

Any disguise requires the same attention to detail as camouflage. In an urban area, there are typically homeless people that can be seen living outside, under bridges and often panhandling at busy intersections. Using these poor souls as an example of observation, ask the following questions:

What types of shoes are typical?

How do they walk?

Do they wear layers of clothing, even if it is hot outside?

How do they carry their possessions? Shopping Cart? Paper bags?

The list of observation questions could be quite long. I have found over the years that regardless of the country, culture or location, there are always pedestrians carrying things around. In the U.S., think about the people you see every day walking down the street carrying a large load. That load could be your equipment. Here are some examples:

- Homeless people pushing carts or towing along suitcases
- College students carrying backpacks
- Business men and computer bags
- Bike messengers and their cargo
- Delivery men and packages
- Maintenance men pushing carts
- Tourists and large camera cases

- Mothers pushing baby carriages and the Dads with diaper bags
- City dwellers pulling along a cart full of groceries

Depending on your age, skills and mission, any of these roles could be used given a proper disguise. One of the easiest examples from the list above to imitate is a homeless person. They come in all ages, shapes and sizes and any mistake or shortcoming in the disguise can easy be explained away by anyone who notices. It is also logical to assume that given a SHTF or TEOTWAWKI environment, wandering homeless people would be even more common.

Some of the list above may not exist in a TEOTWAWKI life. Will students still go to college? Probably not, but the intent of the list above is to provoke thought.

EXERCISE

Play a game of "dress up." Pick one of the disguises listed above, or create one of your own. It should be a role common to your area. Secure the materials or clothing necessary to pull it off, **and do it**. Walk (or ride) around in the disguise.

Make sure you can carry the equipment required. If, for example, it is illegal to have a long gun on your person in your area, substitute something of similar size and weight. You should attempt the various loads described in different sections of this book.

If you are questioned or detected, simply state you are preparing for a costume party or Halloween. That excuse might work, and you may save yourself the price of a costume next October.

9.7 EXAMPLE INFILTRATIONS

9.7.1 SIMULATION I

Our first example involves a post-TEOTWAWKI environment in which there is no law enforcement, no government, or authority. You have been holding your ground at your country home for months. Now food is running low, and unusually cold weather has destroyed the anticipated harvest from your garden.

Passersby have told stories about a nearby town that had been organized by the police chief, and they have commandeered a big distribution warehouse full of food and supplies. These reports also indicate that the townspeople are unwilling to barter or trade. They have set up security and shoot first without asking questions later. You feel this is accurate because one man relaying the story had suffered gunshot wounds. Another source of your information was an entire family near starvation that had been turned away by the town. The ex-police chief, now self-appointed mayor, rules the town with an iron fist, and residents are not allowed to leave. Forced labor is in effect.

Your family is going to be starving soon. All other options have been exhausted.

You decide you are going to investigate the town and see if there is any hope of obtaining food.

9.7.1.1 Simulation I - Plan

The act of observing the town is the goal or mission. You have no other objective except to perform a reconnaissance that may be used for a later infiltration. Our fictitious town is 15 miles away, or roughly a four-hour walk using a cautious, stalking pace.

You decide to leave five hours before dark, arrive in the general area at dusk, stay the night, and perform your observations the following morning. You then plan to egress back home in the late afternoon so as to arrive back before dark.

You know the route via roadways to the town, but have never walked there. Wisely, you determine it best to avoid the roads. The terrain between your location and the town is a mixture of open fields, pasture, and woods. Several farms dot the area. There are small streams on the way, but no major rivers or lakes. A map shows one railway to be crossed and four roads.

Here is a map of the area:

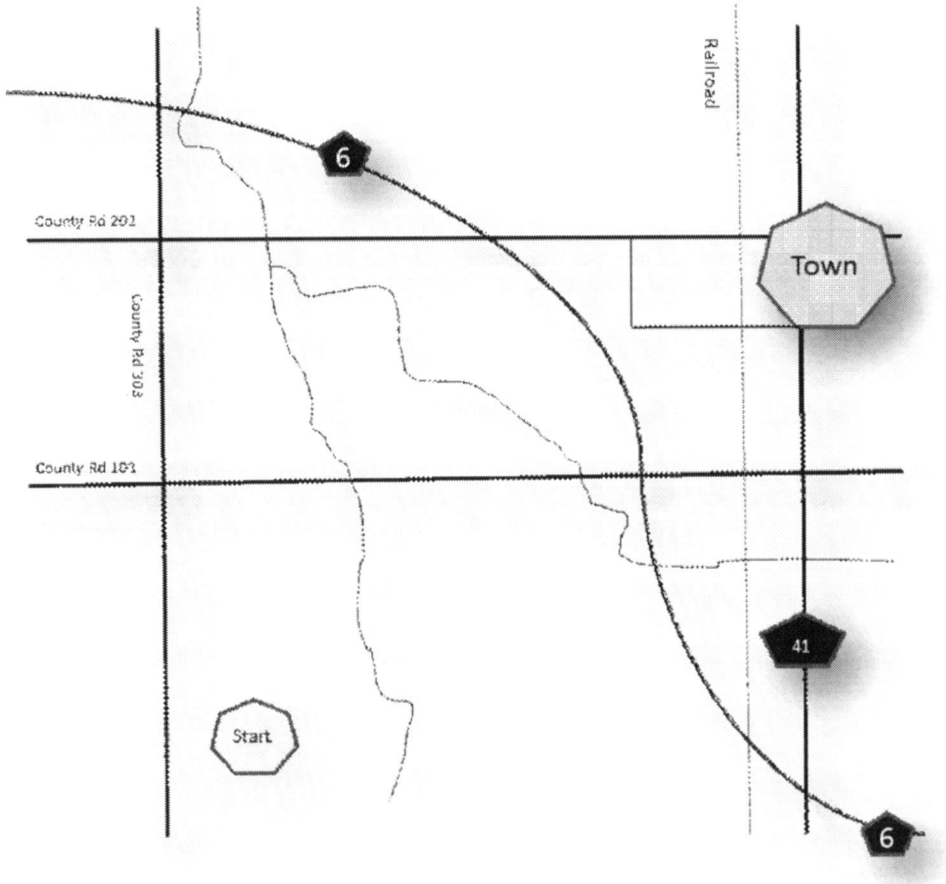

The map shows a few potential trouble areas for the trip. Any crossing of a roadway is dangerous because of the line of sight potential. Anyone watching the roadway can see clearly for miles if the terrain is reasonably flat. Since we want to avoid all contact between our start point and the target, even an innocent bystander can cause issues. Anyone pursuing you later may question spectators later and learn about your direction, path, equipment, and number in your party. Leaving as little evidence as possible is smart in case someone is tracking you.

Major intersections of highways may attract people, such as squatters, homeless or even be a jump off point for organized looters. They should be avoided if at all possible.

Crossing even small streams can be an issue in some climates. Keeping you and your equipment dry and warm should always be a consideration. Larger, deeper waterways can be a real challenge. "Borrowing" a boat is always the best bet, if one can be found close by. Homemade rafts are another option, but despite what can be seen on television, these are not easily or quickly constructed. If you have reason to believe a stream or river is too deep to wade, you have to determine a way to dry your body and equipment after crossing. You should allow for extra time for any water crossing regardless of depth. Even a shallow stream may require going up or down the bank for several hundred yards looking for a good place to cross. Deeper water may require a fire to dry things on the other side. Think this through – fires are one of the easiest ways to be discovered.

Railways pose the same dilemma as highways and roads. They offer a well-placed sentry miles of uninterrupted sight. The section on evading provides recommendations for crossing these obstacles. The good news about railroad tracks is that most people avoid living close by. Also, the tracks often offer better crossing options than the typical surface road due to their construction requirements for drainage and utilities.

After careful consideration and studying all available information, the route to be taken for our example scouting mission is noted below:

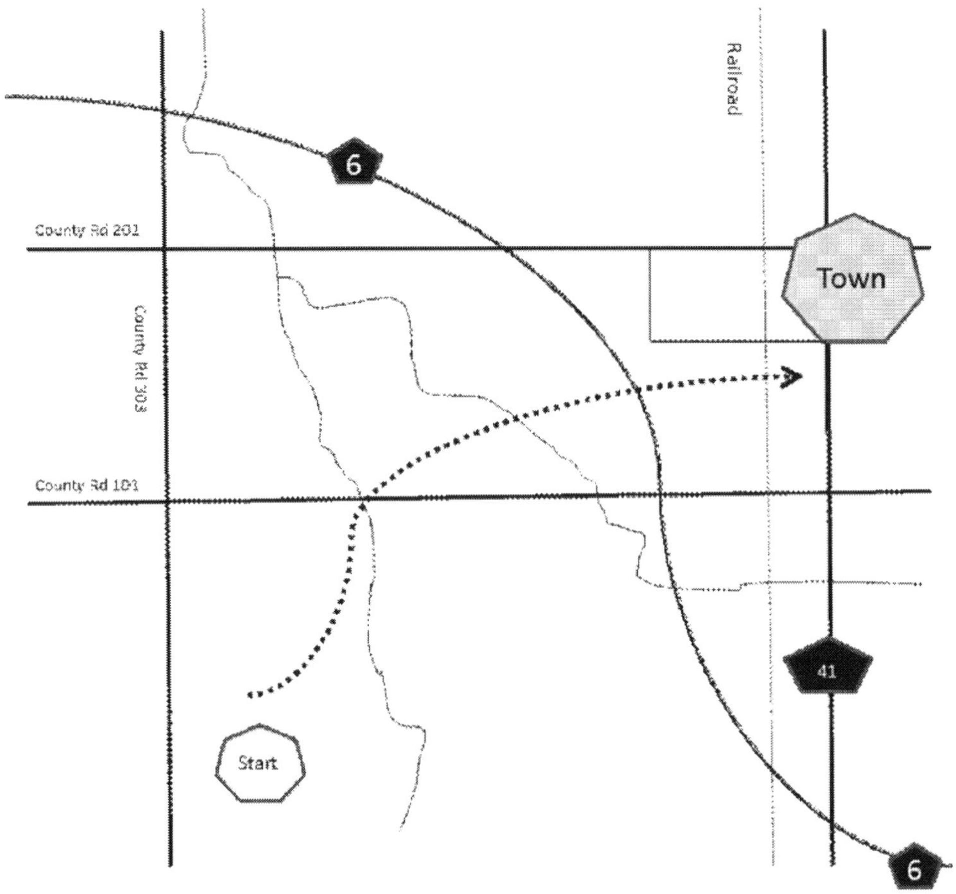

We have a few potential trouble spots on our route. The first is crossing the country road and the stream at their intersection. The justification for picking that spot to cross could be based on several factors, such as the depth of the water or simply "killing two birds with one stone."

The second trouble area is crossing Highway 6 close to town. If the town is truly active with its security, this could be an obvious place for early warning sentries. The reason for selecting that crossing might be "it is as good as any" or be justified because of terrain.

There are always areas that should be avoided because of natural features or obstacles. On our pretend map, one of these is the intersection of the two streams. The area between them is no-man's land for an infiltrator, or anyone else for that matter. If being pursued, this is the last place you want to be "herded into."

It might also appear that going straight west from our jump-off point (start) would seem logical. The issue here is the proximity of the highways (both 41 and 6) to the railway. This would commonly be an area populated with businesses or other folks you would wish to avoid. In addition, if the town has motorized pursuit capabilities, this is the last place we want to be pinned up.

While this example analysis is fictitious, its purpose it to communicate how to analyze an insertion. You need to think about being chased, getting lost, having to navigate at night or during bad weather. A route is like any equipment or plan – it is a series of compromises.

A final note on picking a route: Don't think you are the only one who can read a map. In our example, the people in the town might be using the exact same logic to set up their guards or early warning devices. If you were running the town, wouldn't you?

Given our knowledge of the area, terrain, and limited Intel on the target, we can formulate the following example plan:

There are many different templates for planning. In the field, given you may be referencing the information while walking or in the bush, I prefer a simple, two column, large font format, such as the one shown below.

Operational Step	Notes
16:00 - Departure	5 hours before dark
16:30 - Cross CRoad/Stream	Unknown depth possible issue
17:30 - Cross 2nd Stream	Unknown depth possible issue
18:30 - Cross HW6	May require extra time for good crossing cover

The level of detail you take the time to notate is really a personal preference. Since this type of tactical operation is most likely going to be rare in a post-SHTF life, you should error on the side of more detail versus less.

I recommend you notate the significant steps that either require specific equipment or take more than 10-15 minutes.

20:00 - Eat MRE	Make sure and store packaging
20:30 -Find/Construct Hide	Hide spot critical – must be able to construct in short time before dusk
21:30 -Set Trip wires	Silent trip wires for warning only – no noise makers
21:30 - Sleep	May sleep on ground if hide does not permit stringing of hammock
06:00 – Breakdown Camp	
06:30 - Defecate	
06:30 – 11:00 Build Raft	Observe and not area if task takes less time

Documenting your plan to this level may serve a couple of different purposes later:

(1) You will probably be nervous performing this type of operation. Taking the time in the field to review the plan, read the notes and check your time-table can be reassuring.

(2) If a significant event that causes a delay or detour, you need to see at a glance what steps remain before a given deadline, such as dusk. As an example, let's say you see a hunting party on your insertion route. You decide to avoid them taking a different path, throwing off the schedule by an hour. You could pull your plan and quickly see if you should abort. Perhaps, you were ahead of schedule and can still accomplish your goal. The point is that you should concentrate on the immediate task at hand, and not be trying to calculate deadlines in your head.

So how do we know it takes 30 minutes to prepare an MRE?

How can we plan how long it takes to walk a specific distance carrying our gear?

If you use the **DOPE** from the sections above (*Line Three Checklist*) you will know.

The next step of the plan is to create a master equipment list. Every item should be listed. You should gather all of it together, allocate and balance weight, and walk through the operational steps, making sure you can access each piece as needed.

Below is an example of a master equipment checklist. It shows the 1st, 2nd and 3rd lines of gear separated with weight. This helps with balance and allocation of space in your MOLLE or other load-bearing equipment.

It should be noted that most professionals create their plans on paper or computer spreadsheet and meticulously study each piece of gear and every step.

You should create neat, easily readable forms for your equipment and operational plans. Take the time to weigh your gear and enter the weights. In a TEOTWAWKI situation, you may not have the resources or capabilities to create these valuable tools later.

Equipment Master List 1st Line Gear	Quantity	Line	Weight Each	Total Weight
M4 Carbine	1	1	7.2	7.2
.308 AR10	0	1	8.6	0
M4 Mags	3	1	0.9	2.7
.308 Mags	0	1	1.3	0
Rifle Maint. Kit	1	1	0.8	0.8
Medical Kit	1	1	1.1	1.1
Knife (Fixed)	1	1	1.4	1.4
Flashlight	1	1	0.4	0.4
PVS-14	1	1	1.4	1.4
Dump Pouch	1	1	0.6	0.6
Secondary (pistol)	1	1	2.2	2.2
Pistol Mags	2	1	0.8	1.6
Survival Net	1	1	1.2	1.2
Emergency Food	1	1	0.4	0.4
Water (oz.)	80	1	0.1	8
Poncho	1	1	0.2	0.2
Lighter/Fire Starter	1	1	0.1	0.1
Body Armor	1	1	3.3	3.3
1st Line Total				32.6

Below is the 2nd line gear master checklist:

2nd Line Gear				
Pry bar	1	2	3.1	3.1
Pipe	1	2	1.6	1.6
Pencil/Paper	1	2	0.1	0.1
Rope	1	2	0.6	0.6
Grappling Hook	1	2	0.1	0.1
Chisel	1	2	0.4	0.4
Binoculars	1	2	1	1
Axe	1	2	1.4	1.4
2nd Line Total				8.3

Since we are planning an overnight operation, the 3rd line gear is required:

3rd Line Gear				
Tent	0	3	3.2	0
Sleeping Bag	1	3	1.7	1.7
Mess Kit	1	3	0.8	0.8
Meal (one MRE or equal)	3	3	0.5	1.5
Water Filter	1	3	1.2	1.2
Water Refill (ozs)	20	3	0.1	2
Stove	1	3	0.3	0.3
Hoohaws	5	3	0.2	1
Para-cord (50 ft)	1	3	0.4	0.4
Towels	2	3	0.4	0.8
Paracord (50 feet)	1	3	0.3	0.3
Duct Tape	1	3	0.2	0.2
Shovel	1	3	1	1
Hammock	1	3	1.5	1.5
Spare Batteries (set)	1	3	0.4	0.4
Spare Clothes	1	3	1	1
Pack	1	3	2.2	2.2
3rd Line Total				16.3

Contingencies

- If second stream crossing not accomplished by 18:30, abort.

- If discovered, abort.

- If pursued, use trip wires or hide for overpass, take alternative route back and abort.

Simulation I – Equip

In addition to the equipment required for each step, there are some items that should be included in your equipment list for contingencies. In our example, firing even a single shot is not a good thing, yet we have included several magazines of ammunition. The obvious reason is that we may be discovered at some point and have to shoot our way out.

There are some evasion, security, and egress contingencies that we should **always** be prepared for in a hostile environment. Breaking contact may require the smoke grenades or the anti-personnel booby traps.

The extra MRE is in case we can't ford the streams in a reasonable time, or have to wait on help should we be wounded. Same logic applies to the medical kit and rifle maintenance kit.

Weather, especially in a world where forecasts no longer exist, should always be prepared for, thus, the rain parka. If you are in an environment where extreme cold weather occurs, extra clothing may be required.

Simulation I - Rehearsal

Our plan now provides an equipment inventory list, time line, safety check (for anyone back at the home base), and some contingencies. It also gives us several actions to rehearse:

- Fix a sample meal and make sure all required equipment works, such as the stove (if you already have DOPE on this, plan for that time allocation)

- Make a couple of different types of hides that match the expected territory of the target hide site:

Can you keep your pack and other gear out-of-sight?
Can you use the head if necessary?

- Practice warning only trip wires

- Dig a cat hole; verify hoohaws are moist and usable – can you do your business in your harness, chest rig or vest?

- Verify usage of optic and range estimation using mil-dot or other reticle

- Make a list of everything you want to note about the town. When you build your practice hide, make sure you are comfortable. Practice writing, looking through the scope, and then writing some more. (*Not as easy as it may sound while in a hide position.*)

KEEP TRACK OF THE TIME REQUIRED FOR ALL OF THESE STEPS!

Simulation I – Execute

Any entry into a dangerous environment causes fear. You will find that if you are confident in your equipment, skills, and plan, that fear can be controlled.

As you execute your plan, confidence will build, and fear will subside. Always keep in mind the motivation for your actions. In the example, our family may starve, and that should be enough inspiration for anyone.

Never be afraid to abort and start over another day. The plan above calls for beginning construction of our hide right as the light is fading. If a stream crossing took much longer than anticipated, then the best decision would be to abort. Don't risk bumbling around in the dark (even with NVD this can be a problem) and being discovered.

There is no dishonor in pulling back to try again the next day. It may take two or three attempts to accomplish your goal. Remember that modern military operators have back up. They have lots of people supporting them, and you probably will not. They can afford a higher level of risk than you can because of their training, equipment, and support staff. If they get hurt, they can receive medical care – you probably cannot. Put your ego aside and avoid risk.

9.7.2 SIMULATION II

Our second situation involves scavenging a school. Your family is not going to make it through the winter without restocking supplies. You need to pillage food from a nearby apparently vacant elementary school.

You have already scouted the property, and that trip provided the following intelligence about the target:

(1) The cafeteria has already been cleaned out. The door leading to the kitchen area has been breached, and empty boxes are scattered around the area.

(2) The student lockers and other areas appear to be untouched.

(3) The school is surrounded by homes (H). You know they are occupied because you smelled smoke and have seen flickering candle light.

(4) The creek between the observation hide and the school is 3-4 feet deep and slow moving. It is about 20 feet wide with unknown bottom. The banks were steep, but negotiable.

(5) A dog could be heard barking northeast of the school.

(6) You observed the building for an entire day and did not see any human activity.

(7) The fence is a 4′ chain-link, pipe frame construction. There were no crawl under spots observed. No gates were located.

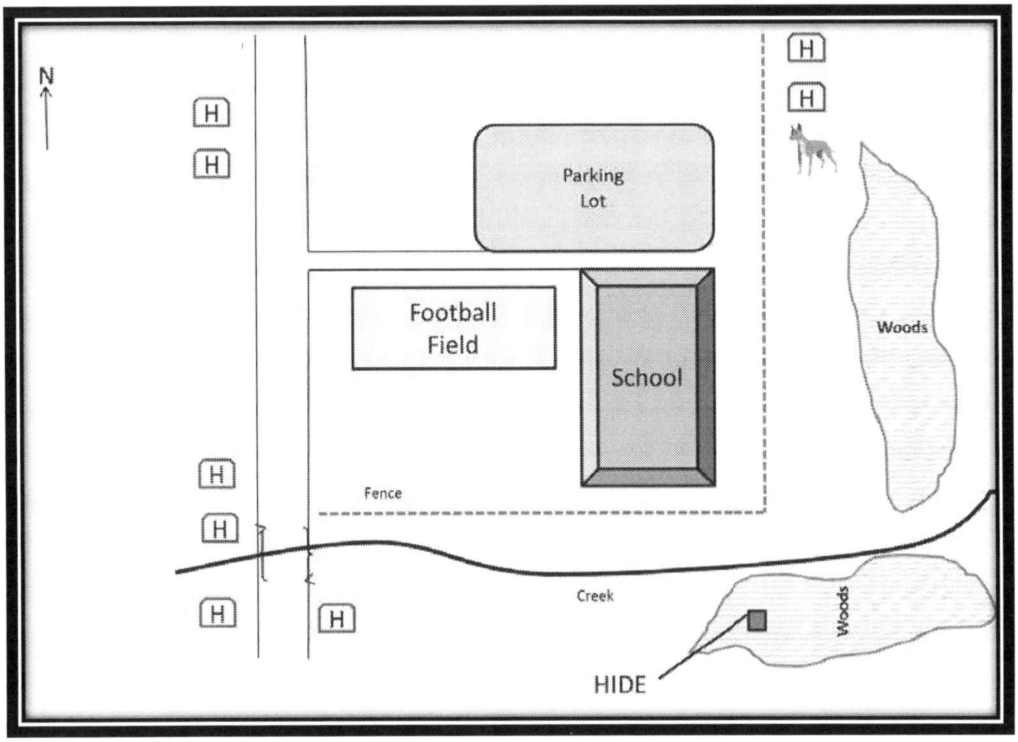

Since there are other people in close proximity, stealth is a requirement. You have to plan to infiltrate and egress without being seen. Since the main store of food appears to have been emptied, you are going to have to spend a significant amount of time searching for any remaining food. Before planning the infiltration, you should determine where your search is going to take place and how long it will take. The first step is to make a list of everywhere in the building there could be food. Aside from the obvious cafeteria stores, mentally go through every place students or faculty might have kept snacks or meals and make a list.

-> Verify kitchen is completely empty
-> Nurses clinic
-> Concessions for sporting events
-> Vending machines
-> Student lockers
-> Teachers' lounge
-> Athletic department

-> Teachers' desks

Clearly, it is going to take an extended period of time to search the facility thoroughly. This is important information for our infiltration because you have to contemplate your own food, water, and equipment needs.

Your plan, equipment, rehearsal and execution are further complicated in this situation because your ultimate goal is to bring back groceries. You have to accommodate additional weight and time on the return trip. You will consume some food and water during the outing, but still have to plan for carrying out more than you carried in.

There are three significant tactical problems with this infiltration:

(1) The homes in the area are occupied, and no one has eaten the dogs. This indicates that the food from the school had kept the local population alive and reasonably comfortable. This probably means they won't take kindly to someone raiding their food supply.

(2) While the creek is no problem to cross on infiltration, it may be an issue on egress with the additional weight of any food scavenged. It is just wide/deep enough to slow down a hasty retreat if discovered. If it has a mud bottom, it could be a serious issue.

(3) The dogs to the northeast are a problem. It is going to be difficult to breach without attracting attention. While most dogs bark at random times, their masters can typically tell when the warning gets serious.

The area directly north of your observation hide is the safest route of approach. There is the least open distance to cover, and it is the furthest point from any population.

The breach should take place at dawn. The first light from the east should provide enough illumination to break into the building as quietly as possible. The plan should allow for the entire day pilfering the school and then egress after dark.

If you are discovered and have to evade, the wooded areas to the south and southeast are the best bets.

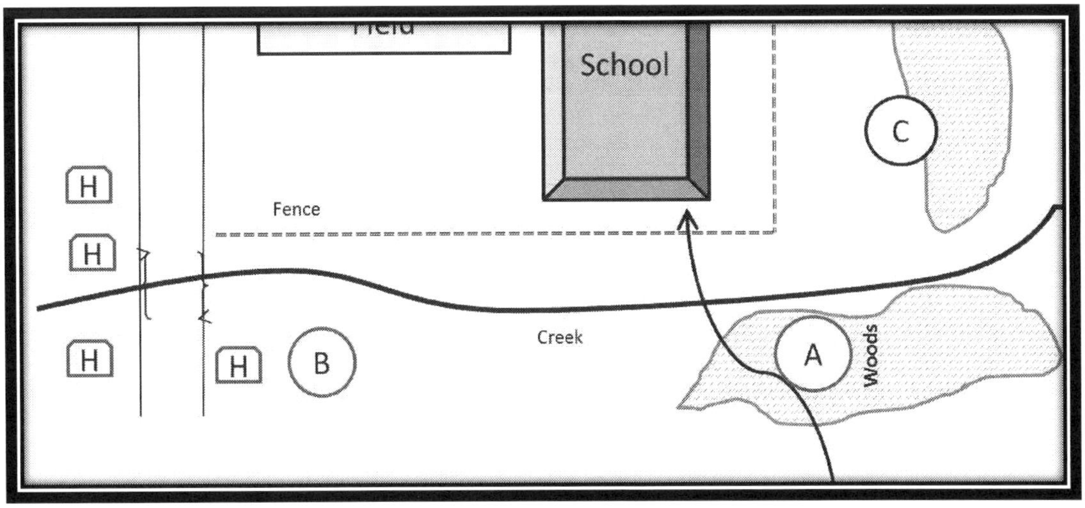

Making multiple crossings of the creek, carrying what will hopefully be several bags' worth of food is simply not an option. The homes (area "B") on the map above have a clear view of the entire area.

It would make sense to build a flotation raft of some sort at the spot labeled "A," and use it to make a single trip across with all of our loot.

Your emergency escape route involves the area labeled "C," which is wooded as well. If you are discovered, the dogs to the north will make little difference. This route is directly away from the majority of the population known to be in the vicinity. Area "C," properly prepared, could provide for setting a fire to slow pursuit if conditions allow.

Simulation II - Plan

This plan would be similar to the one displayed in Simulation I above. You have some additional complexities in that you are going to perform a breach and perhaps build a raft.

The time line for the breach is unknown, and probably impossible to practice or rehearse.

Building the raft can be practiced and timed locally if similar terrain exists.

This simulation is continued in the next chapter on scavenging, and the detailed plan is shown there.

Contingencies

If dogs are loose or make too much racket, abort.

If discovered, abort.

If pursued, exit to the woods directly east of the school; follow the creek until low point or good crossing available.

Simulation II – Equip

At least eight occupied homes were noted within the area. If each has one person capable of fighting, the odds would not be favorable to stand and fight it out. In addition, you are planning on bringing home the bacon, so weight is going to be a factor. You will need to pack enough ammo to break contact, and hightail it home if confronted.

A water crossing, both on insertion and exfiltration, is involved. On the way out, you may be hauling a considerable amount of goods. It would probably be worth the investment in time and additional risk, to construct a raft and make a single crossing to avoid that open space. Few quickly made field rafts will keep their cargo dry, and you have no way of knowing the packaging of any food you do find. Large plastic trash bags, your rain poncho, or other waterproof wrapping should be part of the equipment.

Weather, especially in a world where forecasts no longer exist, should always be prepared for. If you are in an environment where extreme cold weather occurs, extra clothing may be required.

Simulation II - Rehearsal

The plan calls for hauling out as many pounds of food as you can. Assuming the fictitious school contains food, you will have to tote it from the building, across the creek and back home. As the next chapter outlines, there are some options to avoid having to carry all of the bounty the entire trip, but these variations still require that you get the provisions out of the school and away from the immediate area. The section below, *Hauling Off the Goods* provides some options and exercises for this step.

In addition to the rehearsal steps outlined in Simulation I above, you should build a raft and test it at a stream crossing if at all possible. This is really the only new tactical step to execute, so it should be a priority to verify it can be accomplished and timed to see how long it takes to perform the action.

Like anything else, your skills improve with practice. Being within earshot of watchdogs, while potentially hostile people are nearby is not when you want to learn how to construct a raft. Nor do you want to realize the raft won't keep your bounty afloat when you are exiting the school in a big hurry.

Simulation II – Execute

As stated above, there is no dishonor in pulling back to try again another day. Always keep in mind that the priority is your well-being. Perhaps your family will be hungry this winter, but that is in the future. Making a bad decision during a dangerous objective and being injured, captured or killed is NOW.

Never confuse a potential situation with a factual situation. There will be other opportunities to loot, barter, or obtain food. Don't risk everything on a single attempt.

It is often a difficult decision to abort. All of the work, planning, and resources (valuable food in our pretend simulation) that are expended in a failed attempt will not sit well with most people. Keeping a proper perspective is what will keep you alive. Trust your instincts and survive another day.

10. HOW TO SCAVENGE

So you find yourself in a situation where there is no choice but to scavenge. Circumstances and events have unfolded, and now your survival depends on it. Chances are you have run out of something critical, like food or medicine.

Most likely, the easy pickings have already been looted. Being a prepper, you have survived for a time using your own cache. Now the shelves are bare. The problem is that while you were consuming your own goods, those who didn't prepare were out like locusts devouring everything in sight. You are probably late to the game, so we will assume that all of the obvious scavenging locations have already been picked clean.

So where should you go? How do you find what you need? The previous chapters have addressed how to get there and how to get back safely. You need a location to scavenge that no one else has thought of. Assuming that every corner gas station, drug store, and grocery outlet has already been raided down to the floor tiles, you are forced to look where no one else has.

Scavenging is like any other survival activity in that it takes some research, thought and planning. You have prepared food, medicine, ammunition or whatever; why not prepare to scavenge in a long-term post-apocalyptic situation? With a little work and forethought, you can be ready to supplement your supplies and increase your chances of survival.

10.1 SPECIAL EQUIPMENT

- Crowbar or other large prying device
- Nail punch, chisel or large screwdriver (prying device)

- Wire cutters (large enough to sever a common chair-link fence)
- Shovel
- Rope
- Grappling hook
- Survival net
- Fasteners

Optional Equipment

- Bolt cutters
- Shotgun (12 ga. with slugs)
- Rechargeable cordless drill
- Shopping cart, wheelbarrow, wagon or other rolling cargo carrier

The first step in preparing to scavenge involves a simple analysis of what manufacturing companies call the supply chain. How food and other consumables are made, distributed, and sold in our pre-collapse world will become valuable knowledge should everything go to hell. As the old axiom goes, knowledge is power.

10.2 THE MODERN SUPPLY CHAIN

From a business perspective, Supply Chain Management, or SCM, is a science unto itself. Like accounting or engineering, there are professionals in most large firms whose careers focus on the complexities of supply.

For our purposes, you don't need to understand all of the logistics, scheduling and other intricacies of SCM. Your focus needs to be on one specific component – distribution. It is only common sense that the local grocery store receives shipments of bulk goods. Anyone who has ever gone to the market late at night has seen the stockers pushing around pallets of goodies and re-stocking the shelves. It's easy to connect the dots and determine that a large truck recently delivered those pallets to the store. If you looked at the back of the building, you would probably see one or more large semi-trailers backed up to loading docks. But where was the delivery truck loaded? Did it come directly from the "food factory?" Is the food stockpiled at a warehouse somewhere?

In every industrialized country in the world, the distribution of goods is big business. A company that makes canned soup, for example, utilizes distribution not only to ship its finished product to your local market, but also to receive the fresh vegetables from the growers. The next time you are waiting on a train to pass at a railroad crossing there is a good chance some of your food is passing by. The same can be said when you are driving on the road and are annoyed by the slow moving truck in front of you. That's your food blocking the traffic lane.

A simple distribution chain is depicted in the diagram below:

In reality, most distribution systems are far, far more complex. Even with the overly simplified example above, every box and arrow represents an opportunity to scavenge from either the transport or the location.

The diagram below, *copied with permission of Wikipedia,* represents the supply chain for a laptop computer. Even though it looks complex, it too has been simplified. The actual diagram for any computer manufacturer would fill an entire book by itself.

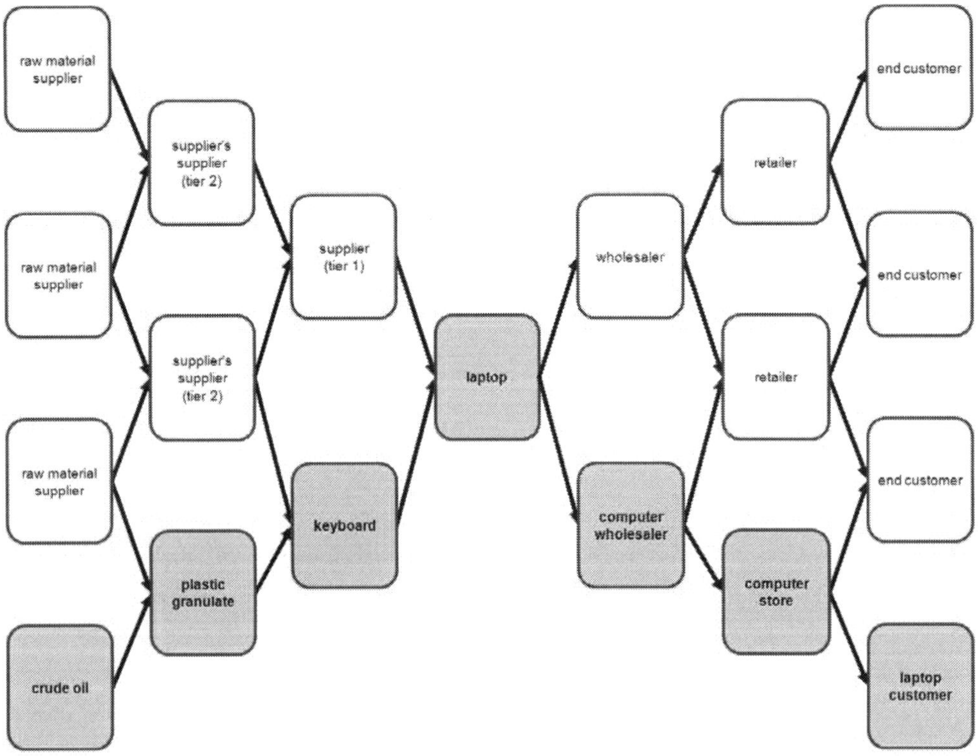

Even if you substituted the laptop with canned soup, the picture would be similar. Every box, arrow, and intersection represents potential opportunity.

So how do you as a prepper know where to find the goods after SHTF? It's really very simple. Just follow these steps:

1. Use the local yellow pages, and look for these listings:
    a. Distributor
    b. Wholesaler
    c. Restaurant Supply
2. Write down the addresses of the businesses listed that are close to your location.
3. Using the same keywords as listed in #1; perform a search of the internet. Again, make note of the addresses.

Depending on the population density of your location, you should be able to create an extensive list of potential food banks. If you live in a larger city, the list could be several hundred entries long. Rural locations may only have a few addresses.

Not every distribution channel can be found by the searches above. Wal-Mart, for example, uses its own distribution network. You will have to dig a little to find a directory of their enormous warehouses, but internet lists of the locations do exist. The same can be said of many national chains, such as CVS or Walgreens. These larger retailers require a little more research to determine where they keep the loot.

One of the simplest ways to determine the location of warehouses is to follow the delivery trucks. Most large outlets take delivery at night, during off peak shopping hours. If you want to pretend to be James Bond, you can wait until a truck has finished unloading and just follow it back to the warehouse. Keep local stalking laws in mind if you decide to endeavor in a little prepper espionage.

You will no doubt find the typical retail outlet has several different distributors.

The goal is to develop a database of potential scavenging locations. In a large metropolitan area, it is probably a safe bet that there are food and medical distribution centers within a short distance of your location. It is also likely that the major facilities will have been cleaned out if you wait too long.

10.3 OTHER POTENTIAL SOURCES

Anyone who has ever worked in an office building knows most companies have a lunch or break room. These normally have food of some sort, if nothing else but a vending machine. Almost every structure occupied or used by people will contain some form of food or water. Here are some examples of where the scavenger of the future may find loot:

- Hot water heaters in homes contain water, but did you know most office buildings have hot water heaters as well? Many taller buildings pump water to holding tanks on higher floors and let gravity provide the pressure for the clients. Even a modest office building will have several toilets and the water in the tank is usable.

- Schools feed hundreds of children one or more meals per day. They also have concession stands, vending machines, and break rooms for the faculty. Many children keep snacks in their lockers as well.

- The supply chain noted above covers warehouses and storage facilities, but at any point in time, there are thousands of trucks, delivery vans, and railroad cars keeping our stores supplied. Would a truck stop be a good place to hunt? What about random trucks that run out of fuel in rural areas?

- Doctor's offices are full of sample medications. These are normally locked away in a centralized closet or storage room. While the typical looter may fill his pockets at the corner drug store, will he think to raid an otherwise uninteresting doctor's office?

- Where does your community have its ambulances repaired or serviced? No doubt, the local EMTs do not completely unload all of the medical supplies from the back just for an oil change.

- If a delivery truck breaks down, where is it repaired? Finding a truck full of breakfast cereal that was towed in because of engine failure would be a bonanza in some scenarios.

- Marinas are full of boats, and many larger vessels have supplies on board. The same can be said of the repair facilities. Don't forget the water, fuel, and medical kits they harbor.

- The average recreational vehicle (RV) will house dry goods at a minimum. Where are RVs parked locally? Where are they repaired in your area?

- Do you know where all of the local orchards are? What about commercial vegetable farms? Fish hatcheries? Scavenging does not have to be related to buildings or structures.

The list of potential locations is practically endless, and that fact alone should be reassuring to the average prepper. The key is to know where your best potential sources of critical supplies are located before you are desperate. Think out of the box for your general area.

Where people normally live, work or play in any given locale, there is little doubt that some form of food, medical supplies or other necessities will exist. You will just have to find them and be the first to do so.

10.4 RECONNAISSANCE

Once you have developed a list of potential locations to pillage, you should use the internet and develop your own personal reconnaissance file for each address on the list. Again, this is fairly simple to do as you can use Google Maps (or any other satellite service) and print off area photos and maps. Most of these free services offer zooming capabilities, so you should create images of the target at different scales.

Satellite reconnaissance can be very useful in countless ways. For example, you can plot a route that offers the most cover or bypasses a housing development between your location and the target.

The next step is to simply drive by the target and take notes or photographs. Again, keep local stalking laws in mind, and be aware that taking pictures of some targets might insinuate criminal activity if you are discovered.

Some people make the mistake of noting alarm systems, cameras and other security features of any given target. This is really unnecessary because your purpose is to raid after the collapse of society, not rob the joint. Almost all modern security systems require electrical power and a police force to respond, and those services will no longer exist after TEOTWAWKI. In addition, if the facility in question is ever robbed, you probably don't want to be caught with detailed information about the security system.

Another point to consider is your bug out plan, location, and route. You may plan to shelter in place, but have an alternative bug out location in mind. You should have information of potential scavenging targets available for the route and BOL on file.

If you are located in an area with an average population density, then you may be able to define a scavenging itinerary that affords multiple opportunities. Leaving your retreat for a pilfering road trip is likely to be **dangerous**, so having multiple potential targets along a predefined route makes sense. Below is a fictitious example:

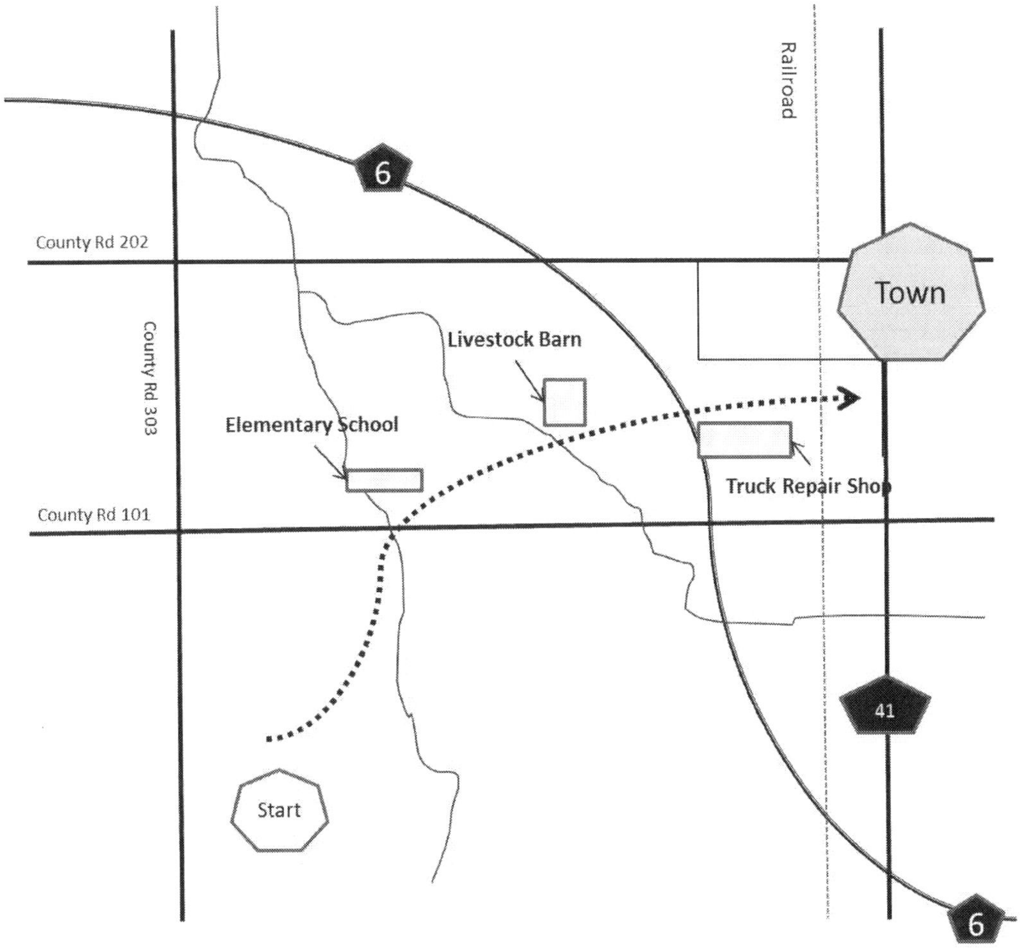

Some people like paper copies of everything, and that is understandable. With the recent development of pad-based computers, it is now a valid option to have all of your information stored in a small, lightweight pad computer and avoid several pounds of books, maps, and recon files. Of course, a solar charging system would offset some weight savings. The thought of replacing 20 pounds of survival books, manuals and other paper with two pounds of electronic gear is attractive. How you store your data is a personal choice.

10.5 TIMING IS EVERYTHING

The decision on when to start scavenging will most likely be a difficult one. In most post-SHTF scenarios, news reports and other reliable information will be sporadic at best. Given a knowledge vacuum, it will be human nature to fall into analysis paralysis. Acting too quickly may lead to arrest, or violent encounters with any remaining authority. Waiting too long might result in everything already being stripped bare. Given that most of us are law-abiding citizens, the conscious decision to take other people's property is not going to be easy. Preppers will be even more vulnerable to procrastination because they won't be as desperate as the average citizen. It might be easy to sit back, consume existing supplies, and wait for things to "get back to normal" or "hold off until things settled down."

In the book ***Holding Your Ground***, there is a detailed description and timeline of how the general population should react given an event. That same analysis can be useful in the determination of the appropriate timing for scavenging.

Scavenging and Time

(post event)

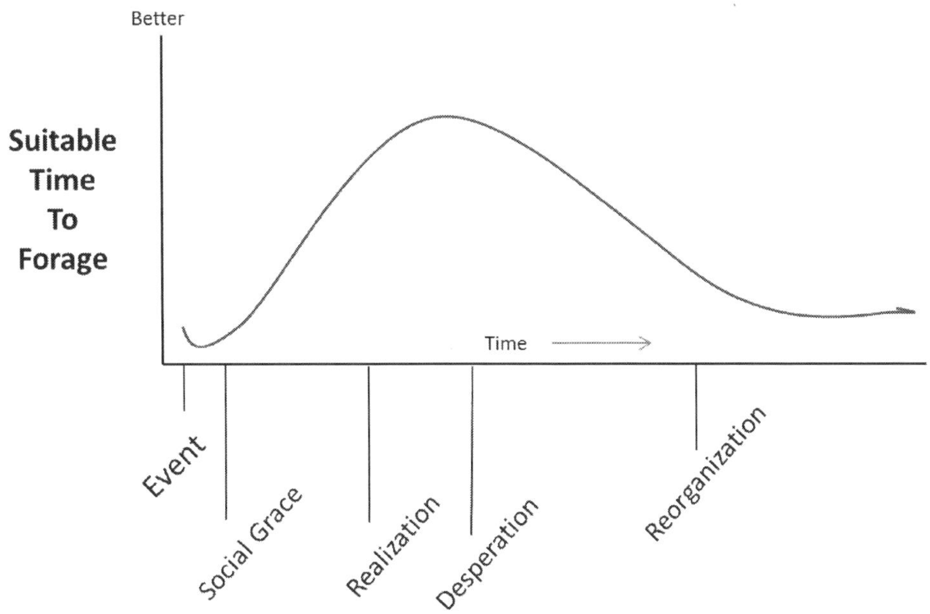

The timeline above depicts the phases likely to be experienced by the general population. A short explanation for each follows:

Event – The trigger or act that initializes a change in society. This could be practically anything, such as an approaching storm, a terrorist attack, or even the outbreak of war.

Social Grace – Historically, when an event has occurred, people have initially banded together to help one another. I call this the *Grace Period,* and the duration is directly related to the severity of the event. As an example, shortly after Hurricane Rita in Houston, the electrical power was out for most of the city. It is well documented that people who had generators would commonly offer to store the frozen food for neighbors who did not have electricity. People shared and helped one another.

Realization – When a severe event occurs, realization will set in. People will become more self-centered or independent. During Hurricane Katrina, this is the stage that general looting began.

Desperation – Again, depending on the severity of the event, desperation will set in when basic services, security, or other needs are not available. The Super Dome in New Orleans after Katrina is a prime example. While initial news reports of murder, rape and other illegal behavior were greatly exaggerated, the more time that expired, the more desperate those people became.

Reorganization – At some point, humans will organize. We always have. The amount of time that expires between desperation and reorganization will depend on the severity of the event. This means that you can establish parameters within your plan. You will not be on red alert forever, and that is important to know.

Clearly, the best time to start scavenging is at the end of the social grace period, and prior to complete desperation. Unfortunately, it may be impossible to accurately judge what is happening around you out there in the real world.

There are very few historical examples of out-and-out looting in the United States, which can be attributed to a true survival situation. One valid case study is New Orleans, after hurricane Katrina. Research indicates that not a single person was prosecuted for stealing food or medical supplies in the city proper. A prepper, holed up in New Orleans, could have made an early decision to scavenge and not faced punishment after order was restored. It is reasonable to assume the same in most SHTF situations. Should authority or government be restored at a later date, people who pilfered food will probably not be convicted by a jury of their peers.

This is not to say that you should start raiding the local grocery store at the first sign of trouble. Acting too soon, perhaps due to inaccurate information, could have serious consequences. Not only would any existing government or law enforcement be a potential issue, there could be elements of the population initially prowling for non-essential goods, like alcohol, tobacco, or electronics. These looters will probably not realize all of those items are soon to be virtually worthless, and they could easily be violent. In New Orleans, there ***were*** prosecutions for stealing jewelry and electronics.

At the other end of the spectrum, waiting too long to replenish your supplies has obvious implications. Eventually, even the most inaccessible sources will be found by a desperate population.

There are so many variables involved, it becomes impractical to develop any realistic guidelines on when to evolve from a "law abiding prepper" to a "survive at any cost scavenger." There are, however, some recommendations based on common sense and an honest evaluation of the situation:

- You don't want to be the first to begin raiding, and you don't want to be the last one there either. If you see positive evidence that things have degraded to the point of looting, such as people walking down the street carrying goods, then you probably want to pay attention.

- Evaluate the likelihood of any form of government or legitimate authority regaining control. If, as in the case of New Orleans where the situation was regionalized, chances are order will be restored in a short period of time. Wait it out.

- Your personal situation and level of desperation should be a major factor. If you have months of food on hand, then waiting a few days to see what develops is probably wise. If the shelves are barren, you might want to start planning your first forage.

- The status of you (or your group) should be taken into consideration. If you wait until everyone is hungry and weakened, then the chances of success are lower.

- The absence of law enforcement is a key indicator. Like New Orleans, if the local police no longer have a presence or control in your area, then it may be time to act. It is realistic to predict that there will be a gap between local authorities losing control and the deployment of any federal troops or National Guard. The military cannot respond to most situations immediately. One serious piece of advice – don't attempt to loot in areas controlled by the military – the threat of "looters will be shot on sight" is real.

I will personally "pull the scavenging trigger" sooner rather than later. You can have the best plan ever created, but if everything has already been plundered, it won't do you any good. You can be the most dangerous man still walking, but if it's all gone, you will starve.

10.6 BREACH AND ENTRY

Once you have made it to the location you intend to pilfer, most likely you are going to have to breach and enter a building of some sort. As an honest, law-abiding citizen, you probably have little real world knowledge about entering a locked building. In a SHTF situation, however, your life may depend upon your ability to do so.

Consider the logistics involved now. In a post-TEOTWAWKI world, alarm systems should not be an issue. What may give you more trouble than anticipated are common doors and windows, especially on industrial or commercial buildings.

Common sense adds another layer of difficulty to this task. You should **not** leave any evidence of your presence. If you discover a good cache of food, the chances are you won't be able to carry it all, (see the next section) and you may want to return later for another load. If the facility were untouched when you got there, you improve the chances your presence will not be detected if you leave things looking like they did when you entered. You may even want to add security around the stash.

There are several tools that can come in handy for making your way into a building. A crow bar, bolt cutters, and cordless electric drill come to mind. Hollywood has schooled us that the more sophisticated thief may include glasscutters and lock picks, but those devices require skill and practice and have little value in this instance.

For clarity, we will address different methods of breaching as two categories, destructive and non-destructive.

10.6.1 DESTRUCTIVE BREACHING

In this context, the term destructive is used to describe methods of entry that result in permanent damage to the structure, and is a last resort. Bent doors, broken windows, caved in walls, etc. Destructive breaching is typically faster and louder than non-destructive approaches. Nothing is gained by the destruction of a solid structure.

One of the most commonly used destructive methods is called shotgun breaching, involving 12 gauge shotgun slugs being used to blow a door off its hinges, or destroy the wooden door frame housing the lock(s). After the breach, the door is destroyed for all practical purposes – sometimes the entire doorframe.

Here are some example destructive breaching techniques:

Prying or leverage based entry – where a crowbar or other prying tool is used to defeat a lock or latch.

Explosive entry – The military has some specialized breaching charges that can take about any door off of its hinges. Some of these devices can even make a new doorway through a solid wall, which is often called mouse holing. Shotgun breaching is part of this category.

Battering entry – Developed by American troops in Iraq, the front bumper of a vehicle is used as a battering ram and basically pushes a heavily reinforced door inward. Breaking out a window is also considered a form of battering entry.

Towed entry – Everyone remembers the old cowboy movies where the outlaws rescued their comrade from the jailhouse by tying a rope around the window bars and pulling them off with their horses. This would be an example of a towed entry. A modern day equivalent would involve tying a rope around the subject and using a vehicle to tow it open. Any method that pulls open an entry would be classified as towed.

Cutting entry – A new favorite of criminals, this method involves using power tools to cut through a roof or wall of a structure. This method takes some amount of time to accomplish and is normally applied to roof entries. If a cutting torch is used, this method is often called thermal breaching.

There are advantages and disadvantages to using destructive techniques:

Advantages	Disadvantages
Typically the fastest way into a structure. This is why these methods are popular with law enforcement and military. They want the door off and the stick pouring in.	Normally loud and noisy. Everyone in close proximity will know someone is busy nearby.
Will disable or stun anyone on the other side of the door.	Leaves evidence that someone breached. Doors will be bent, burnt or hanging by the hinges.

10.6.2 NON-DESTRUCTIVE BREACHING

Sometimes referred to as quiet breaching, non-destructive techniques are described below:

Lock picking or Lock bypass – Sometimes referred to as mechanical breaching, a professional can pick or bust a lock without leaving any sign of the activity. Being able to pick a lock takes a lot of skill and practice. Not a technique the typical prepper usually has any experience with.

Blocked Closure – Another technique that is probably not useful for preppers. An example of this method would be placing a large wad of bubble gum or putty in a lock mechanism to prevent it from engaging the bolt. In order to block a closure, you must have access while the door is unlocked.

Trap Doors – If you can enter a structure via the roof or other unobvious entrance, it might be called a trap door.

10.6.3 PLANNING A BREACH

It is logical to assume that the vast majority of scavenging will be done inside of some sort of structure or building. It is important to perform a detailed analysis of the structure and the surrounding area before determining the entry method.

Don't make the mistake of thinking in two dimensions when formulating your plan. Consider any structure as a box with sides, a top, and bottom. You can open the box from any of these perspectives.

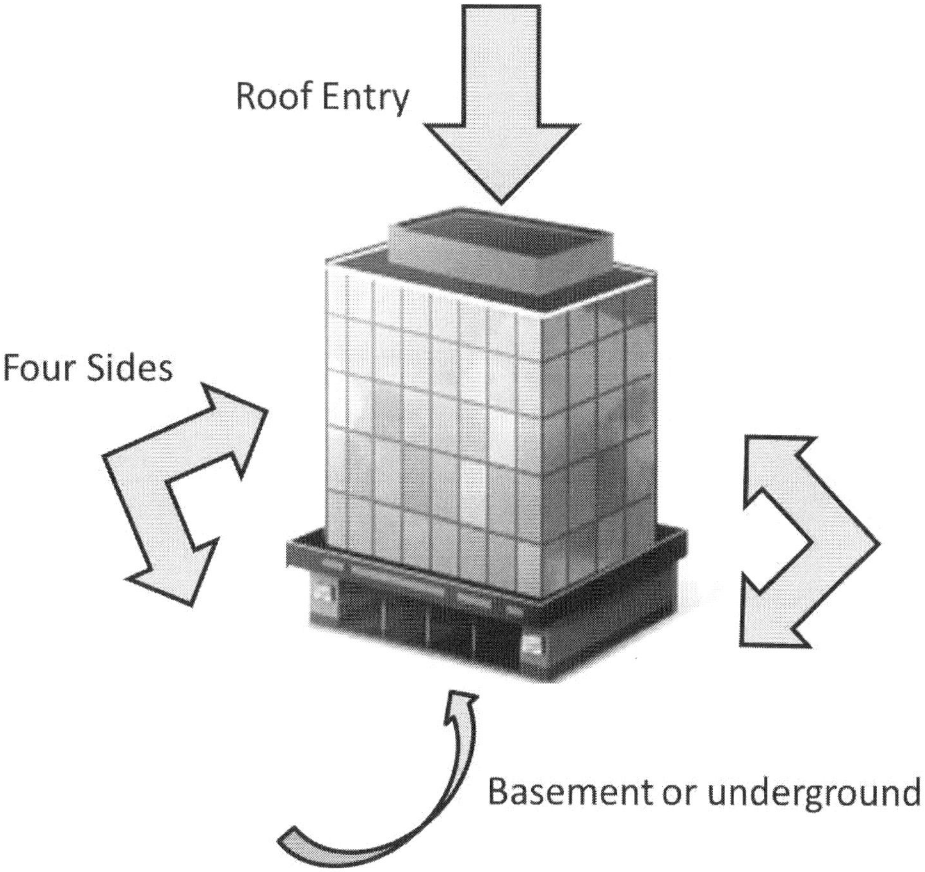

While doorways and windows are obvious entry points, don't overlook the top (roof) and bottom (basement) of any structure. These two options can have several advantages, such as being less visible to the surrounding area.

Many rooftops are easily accessible because they contain the air conditioning or other utilities required for the structure. Any mechanical components on the roof require maintenance, so access is typically designed into the structure. For taller buildings, the access is probably available from inside of the structure. For single or two story buildings, the access is most likely from the outside of the structure via ladder or fire escape.

Vents, air conditioning ducts and other rooftop features can provide an easy method of non-destructive breaking and entering. While you may have to imitate a Hollywood movie cat burglar and crawl through a few air ducts, this method is worthy of consideration if the area demands a stealthy breach.

A few notes about rooftops:

- Be extra cautious of silhouetting and movement. You are elevated and can be seen from considerable distances.
- If discovered by hostiles, being on a rooftop equates to being trapped.
- Before breaching via the roof, consider how you are going to get your loot down.
- Make sure the roof area cannot be observed by taller structures in the area unless you intend to operate at night.

Basements and sewers (or other tunnels) can also provide a valid entry point. As with rooftop breaching, you must consider how you are going to haul off the bounty. Sub-terrain access points normally provide better cover than the wide-open spaces of the skyward options. Many office buildings have parking garages that are attached via underground walkways. These can be an excellent avenue for a destructive, noisy admittance.

10.6.4 LEVERAGE

One of the most common methods of breaching involves the utilization of leverage. While most preppers don't have a lot of experience breaking and entering (we hope), the act is not overly complex and with the right tools can be accomplished quickly.

To begin, a little understanding of basic physics helps. Archimedes is credited with first documenting the *Law of the Lever*. As a prepper, you need to understand one basic premise of using a lever:

The longer the lever is from the fulcrum (pivot point), the more force is applied to the object to be leveraged.

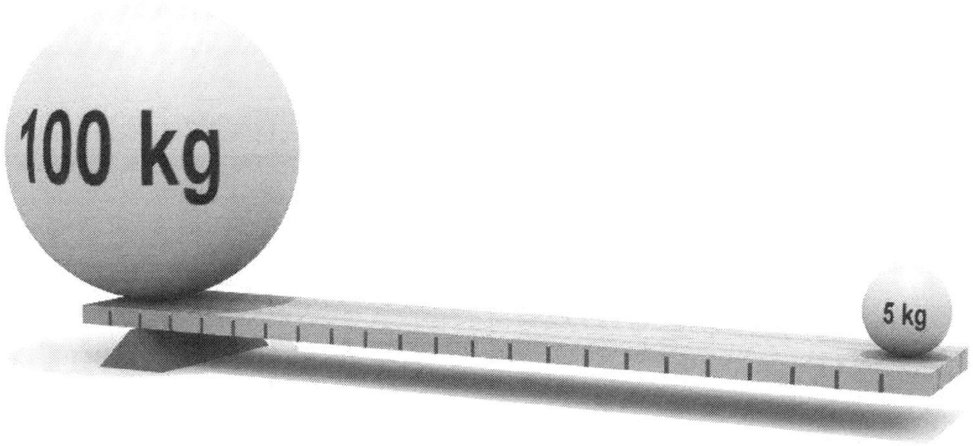

So what does that translate into for a prepper who is faced with a heavy steel door? The longer the handle on your prying tool, the more leverage you can apply against the door.

Typical hardware store pry bars come in many shapes and lengths. The longer the tool, the heavier it becomes. This flies in the face of our rule about weight as well as carrying it around in a concealed fashion. One solution is to acquire a shorter pry bar and also carry along an extension handle. A common length of steel pipe works great and can also be used as a hammer for driving in a nail punch or chisel. In the picture below, option B will provide more leverage than option A. In addition, option B can be stored easier and weighs less.

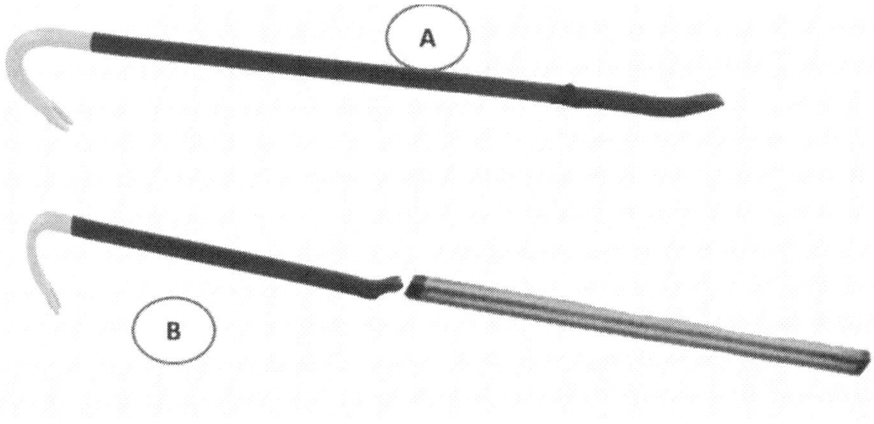

Remember, you are going to have to carry your entry tools in addition to other equipment. If you do find loot, it has to be carried back as well. Weight is everything.

A note about pry bars: For general breaching, avoid models that have the hooked end. The candy cane shape is for pulling nails, which most likely will not be used while scavenging.

There is no big secret or proper technique for prying. Wedge the sharpened tip into a door jam, hinge, or wherever it will fit and apply force – as much force as you can.

The chisel, listed above in the equipment section, can be used to make an opening for the pry bar if the door or window seal is too narrow. Use the pipe or axe as a hammer.

The typical padlock is no match for a well-leveraged pry. If you can manage a fulcrum and enough force, something will eventually break.

Some people think bolt-cutters are a better tool to be used against a padlock. This may or may not be true. It is only common sense that a pry bar is a more flexible tool and will afford you more options for busting into buildings.

10.6.5 HYDRAULICS

A common vehicle tire jack can be an excellent breaching tool in some situations. It is one of the few destructive options that should be relatively quiet. Depending on the scenario and event, it is valid speculation that abandoned cars will be available. Most should contain a jack in the trunk.

Even the stoutest iron bars, often called a security cage are no match against a jack.

Small hydraulic jacks are also available at many retail outlets. Even the smallest are very powerful, yet also heavy. The picture below shows a two-ton model that can be purchased for less than $15.00. It weighs about three pounds.

There are frame jacks, scissor jacks, bottle jacks...you name it. People have been utilizing hydraulics for years to apply force.

The most difficult part of using a jack is the clearance between the head and the base. Many door handles will simply snap off, and depending on the quality and type of lock may not produce the desired result. The key is to jack the entire door inward or upwards. The diagram below shows two different angles of attack that might be effective.

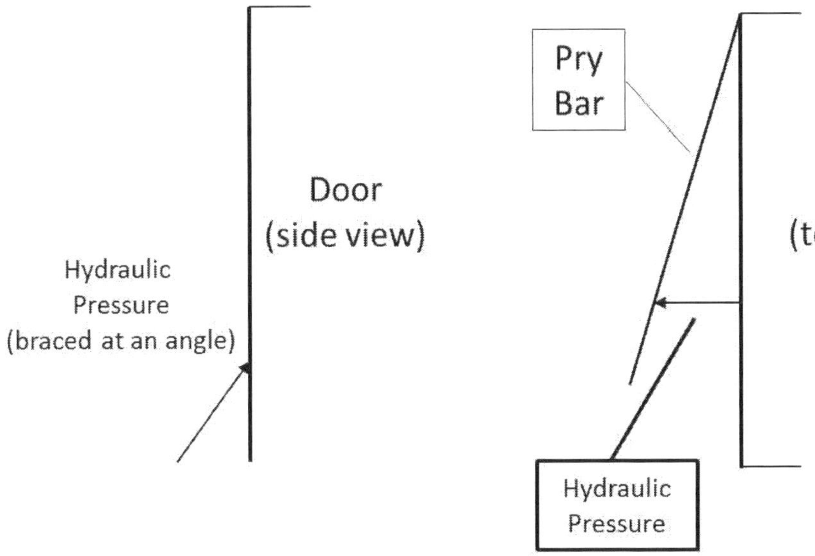

One of the most versatile hydraulic tools is called a farm jack (shown below). These handy units are used by farmers who have multiple sized tires and vehicles to maintain.

This need for flexibility has resulted in a product that is similar in design to the equipment used by fire and rescue teams to breach mangled automobiles. One word of caution about farm jacks – they are very heavy.

As with all equipment, weight should always be a consideration. Hydraulic equipment is always heavy and often bulky. However, if you know of a target that is likely to contain whatever you need, and it is a tough nut to crack, consider hauling over a good jack.

The angle, surrounding frame, and type of door will dictate success or failure using hydraulics as a breaching tool.

10.6.6 CLIMBING

To access a rooftop, second story window, or even to hide in a tree (not recommended), you may have to climb. Unless you are in good physical condition or climb for recreational activity, ascending without elevator buttons can be a challenge.

Many adults cannot pull themselves up a rope, let alone repel or use other advanced climbing techniques. This lack of upward mobility somewhat limits your options to access certain places. It could also mean that a facility denying ground level accessibility could contain the king's ransom in loot, as no one can get to it.

Since you can't eat them, there is no reason to predict ladders will be in short supply if it all falls apart, but these tools are heavy and difficult to conceal. Climbing onto a roof using a ladder would bother me, as it would be easy for someone to come up behind me or take the ladder away, leaving me trapped.

Traditional rope ladders are an option, but they are large, bulky, and difficult to secure. If you are standing at ground level, throwing a rope ladder up to a rooftop is next to impossible. Using a rope ladder to access a second-story ledge or balcony is even less probable.

One valid option for those preppers in reasonable physical condition is to make what I refer to as a snake ladder. You won't find that term in any military technical manuals – I just made it up long ago.

The first step in constructing a snake is the grappling hook or catch. You can purchase commercial grappling hooks designed specifically for climbers, but I have found them to be expensive, heavy, and bulky. If you intend to climb a lot, they might be worth the investment. I have found that a common, 18 gauge treble fishing hook will do the trick pretty well and could make an argument that the sharp pointed barbs will actually catch and hold on some surfaces better than a blunt ended grappling prongs. These fishhooks are small (in comparison), lightweight and very inexpensive.

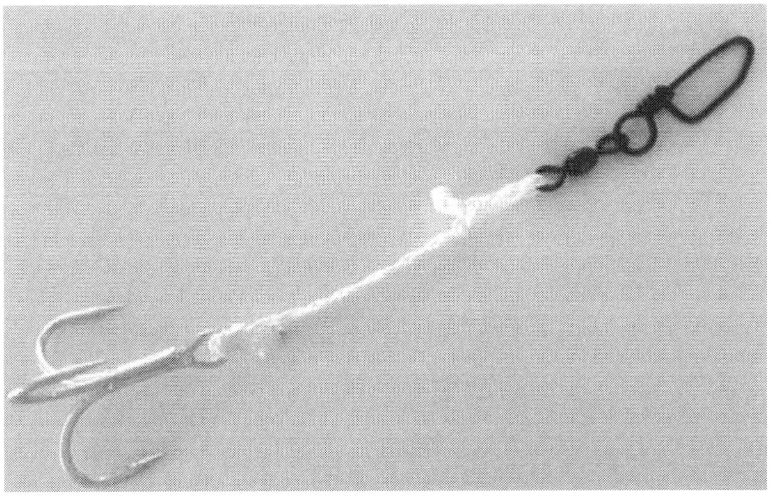

While you are at the local fishing tackle store, pick up a ball bearing swivel (as shown above) rated for 300 pounds or more. Your final purchase at the bait supply should be some 400-600 pound bow fishing line (used to fish via a bow and arrow). I prefer this line to normal Para cord (sometimes called 550 cord) because it is designed to resist wear and tear while in the eyelets of fishing tackle. Any equipment designed to catch 600-pound fighting fish will no doubt hold a 200+-pound man.

You want the swivel for two reasons. The first is that it makes disconnecting the hook from the rope quick and easy. The second is that it helps with tangles and knots while in use. This small grappling hook will fit inside of virtually any pouch. If you wrap some tape around the hook points, you can even store it in your pants pocket.

The next step is to secure your rope to the grappling hook. Anyone who has ever secured a fishing knot knows how to do this. If you are not a fisherman, any knot that is secure will do the trick. The internet if full of videos and diagrams on knot tying.

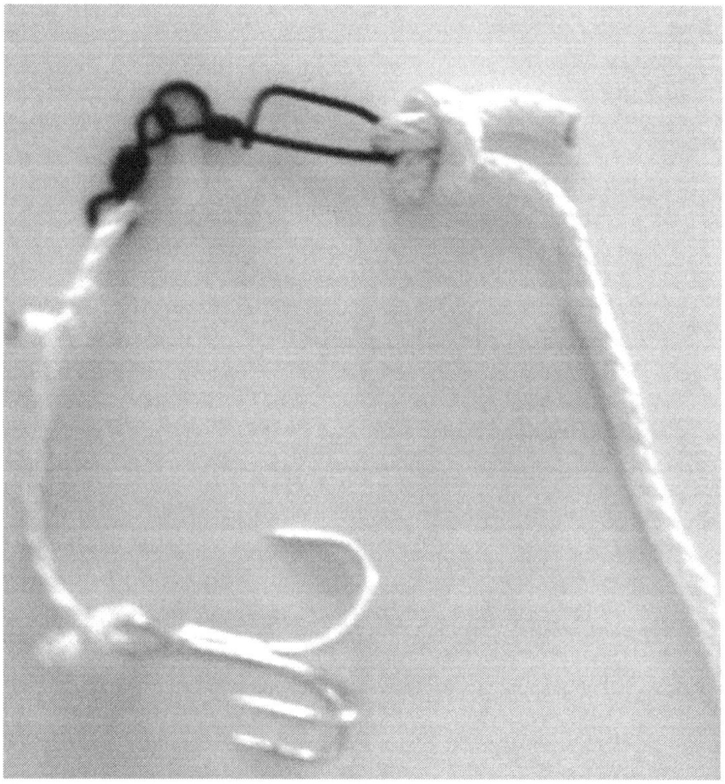

Now is a good time to bring up the subject of rope size and climbing. Even the strongest people have difficulty pulling their weight up a thin rope. There just isn't enough surface area to work well with the human hand. In reality, a single strand of Para cord, rated at 550 pounds of tensile strength, would support a person and gear. It is unlikely you will see anyone using it as climbing rope. On the other hand, carrying around a one-inch thick climbing rope would waste a lot of space and weight. Like so many things involving survival gear, you have to compromise.

It is possible to tie "loops" into the rope and make your own foot and hand holds. I have never had much luck with this method for a couple of different reasons. The first problem is getting your boot into the footholds. Unless your rope if very thick (defeats the purpose), it is difficult to insert a boot. The second issue becomes removing your boot to go to the next step. Finally, a thin rope loop tends to squeeze your hand as you pull up your weight. This can cause issues with your grip and be painful.

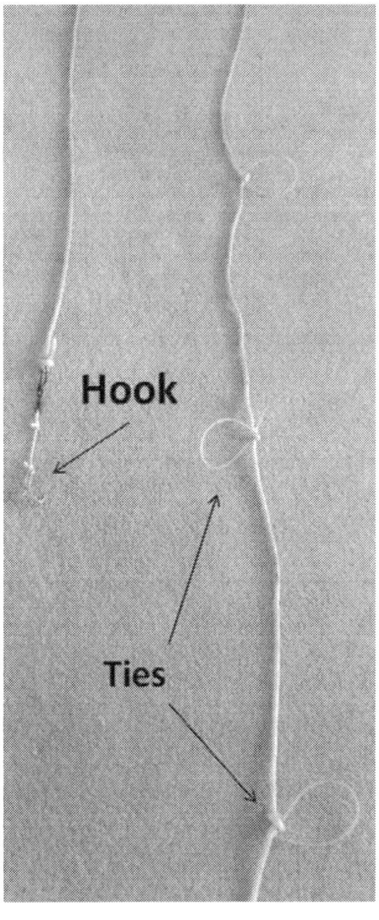

One option I have found that works reasonably well while developing the snake is using reusable gear ties from my survival net to create steps. You basically take reusable gear ties or heavy-duty nylon ties and hook them through knots every 18 inches or so. A few words of advice on this method:

- Use the biggest nylon ties (sometimes-called zip ties) you can find - not only for strength, but also for getting your boot toe in and out. For a 200lb man, they should be about .5 inches thick and 24 inches long. ***TEST THEM*** *at a low height, just to make double sure.*

- The knot in the rope is the key. Most knots will slip as you put weight on them. Experiment with a few different methods.

- Secure the bottom, or anchor, of the rope if at all possible.

- Wear gloves!

- When you are finished, loosen the rope knots before you cut or remove the steps.

- Take off your pack and remove as much gear as possible to reduce weight. I climb with my rifle (double check the safety) slung over my back. Tie your pack or other equipment to the bottom of the rope so you can pull it up to you. This can also serve to anchor the bottom of the line so it does not swing and twist as much.

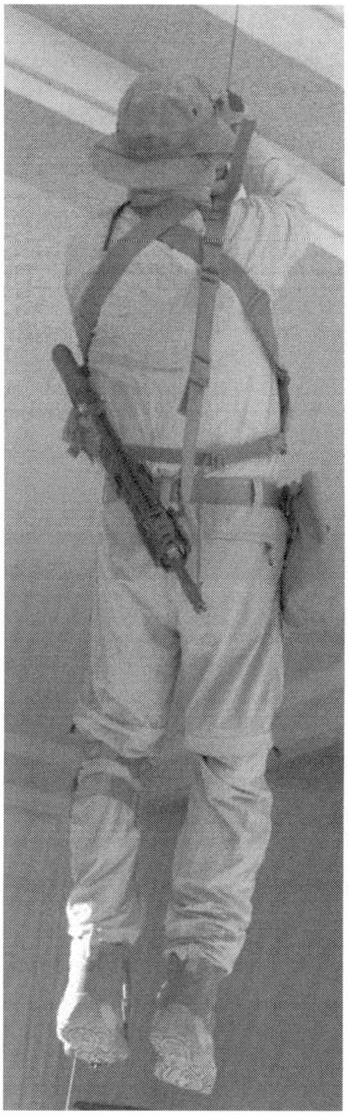

10.7 SYSTEMATIC LOOTING

There is a strong possibility that you will have to search any facility for extended periods of time while scavenging. The typical office building or school contains many thousands of square feet, and that can take time to explore thoroughly.

It is also likely that you will have your own personal security to worry about. It could be a very uncomfortable situation if other looters were to show up while you are pillaging.

A study of the commando raids of WWII provides some recommendations as to the proper methods to search, collect, and triage items discovered during your shopping spree.

The first priority after gaining entry is to establish security. Assuming you are alone, this can be difficult to accomplish in a large facility. The following system is recommended:

(1) Secure your entry point as best as possible. You can never be sure if someone watched you enter and may decide to follow. At minimum, make sure someone following you will make noise in order to provide warning. A trip wire with some sort of noise making device is often a good option. (*see Random Thoughts on Hiding above*)

(2) Verify no one else is already in the structure. This effort can be dual purpose, as you need to scout the inside of the structure in order to prioritize your search areas.

(3) Establish an alternative exit point if possible. You do not want to become trapped inside of the structure with only one way out.

(4) Pick a concealed area close to your primary exit point for a cache. You will need a closet, small room or other area where bounty can be stashed, sorted, and prioritized after you have concluded your search.

(5) If the structure has a complex floor plan, make a sketch. Mark walls, turns, or doors as you pass by during your search.

(6) Work from the inside toward the outside of a large structure. Work from the top floors down on a multi-floor building. Keep in mind that the longer you are in the area, the more likely it is you will be discovered and may have to escape. It is only logical to assume escape will be easier from a lower floor.

(7) As you find booty, move it to the cache point and return to your search. In a very large building, you may need more than one cache (triage) point.

(8) Determine how you are going to transport your loot after prioritizing.

(9) Scout the exit path thoroughly. If a hostile saw you enter the building, it would be smart to let you do all the work and then ambush you on the way out.

There are several potential elements that can turn a successful raid into an absolute disaster. While some circumstances may be no fault of your own, there are some preventative measures that can minimize the chances of failure. Mostly, strong mental discipline is the key:

(a) Don't be greedy. Wasting time and energy trying to prioritize which bounty to return home with is almost as bad as trying to carry back too much and slowing yourself down. The section below contains recommendations on this topic.

(b) Rather than enter into "analysis paralysis" while choosing items to haul back, pick the highest value items, and hide the rest.

(c) Secure your loot well. You may have to move quickly on the way back home, and to drop breadcrumbs for anyone following you would not be wise.

10.8 HAULING OFF THE GOODS

The average, non-motorized prepper can carry only so much loot on foot. If the insertion or egress is potentially dangerous, the amount of goods that can be hauled off is reduced even more in order to focus some resources on the ability to fight or retreat quickly.

At first glance, the concept of wandering around the post-collapse world while scavenging for food does not appear to be an effective survival technique. If you are fully equipped to breach, fight and egress, then you are going to be able to carry 20-30 pounds of food – at most. Now, if you and your family are starving, 20-30 pounds of groceries may seem like the mother lode, but it won't last long. We are simply an animal that eats a lot.

This problem is quickly solved if you have a group of co-looters, or one of earliest inventions – wheels.

Any of the following can be used to tote away your bounty:

- A vehicle of any kind

- A shopping cart or wagon

- A dolly with crates or boxes

- A stretcher (can be dragged along by one person)

- A survival net (can be dragged along by a single person)

EXERCISE

Take your survival net and cutting tool (knife, ax, or machete) to a remote area with terrain similar to where you will be living post-collapse. Find something reasonably heavy to simulate your loot. Rocks, a fallen log, a bag of sand or even small children can be used. I have used my full bug out-bag (60+ lbs.) as practice bounty, but this is cheating in a way as I would normally be wearing some amount of that gear.

Cut two support poles if in a wooded area (cutting down saplings is illegal in most parks) and weave them along each border of the survival net. *Hint – it is easier to both cut and weave three or four smaller, pencil-sized poles than a single large one.*

Attach your rope through the net and attempt dragging the simulated load of goodies around for a while. This method is also good practice for using the survival net as a stretcher.

In addition, you can use the survival net in a fashion similar to a "Santa Claus" bag. Make a sack by weaving your rope through all four sides of the net to cinch the sack shut when tightened. Pile your loot in the middle of the net, and pull the rope tight to make a nice bundle.

Paratroopers learned a long time ago to balance their weight front and back. Using this tip, stress on the back muscles and spine is reduced during a long walk. If you are carrying a heavy pack and believe it unlikely you will need your weapon quickly, consider tying your looters bag so it is on the front.

Most folks have seen pictures of people in third world countries carrying baskets of food or even water on their heads. Depending on your loot's shape and size, this is a proven method as well.

Another method is the bindle, but very little weight can be carried this way. Hobos were often referred to as bindle sticks because of their method of carrying their few worldly belongings tied in a handkerchief on the end of a stick.

Finally, there is the shoulder pole, sometimes called a rack stick. Basically, a pole with a weight on each end is carried across the shoulders. This method is commonly used throughout the world. Your survival net can be used to create the basket at each end of the pole.

You will no doubt find you can carry twice as much weight by dragging it along as compared to carrying the bag over your shoulder if the terrain is cooperative.

Another valid concept is "the squirrel." For example, let's say you find a warehouse full of protein bars. There are dozens of full boxes. It is impossible to carry them all, and you are concerned others may find the stash.

If the situation allows, you could act like a squirrel and hide as many boxes in as many locations as you can find close by. Just as our furry mascot, if another animal finds one of your hiding places, you still have plenty left for the winter.

Finally, you should consider hiding the bounty in plain sight. For example, if you entered via the roof of the warehouse, could you manage to store several boxes on the roof until you can safely return later? Would anyone think to look up there? If you breached the facility using a non-destructive method, you might have a great hiding spot just a few feet away from the goods.

10.9 THE SCAVENGING SIMULATION

In the chapter on Infiltration, Simulation II, we had scouted and planned to scavenge a school building. As a result of the exercises associated with those chapters, the route, insertion, and egress have all been planned. Continuing those scenarios, how could you search the entire school for supplies? How are we going to escape with the provisions?

The exact same methodology used in previous topics should be used here as well. A plan should be created, followed by equipment selection, rehearsal, and finally execution.

There are several unknowns that cannot be thoroughly practiced in this pretend exercise. How long will it take to breach the lockers if they are closed and locked? How many doors are locked within the school?

The answers to all of these questions cannot be determined until we are physically within the facility. When faced with so many unknown factors, there are two important aspects to always keep in mind:

- Plan to accomplish what is known first.

- Whenever possible, choose the path of least resistance.

This logic can be applied to the schoolhouse search in many ways. For example, we don't know the status of the student lockers. There may be hundreds of locked doors requiring noisy breaches. The results may be a few snacks or rotten lunch boxes hidden among the school supplies. A lot of effort, time, and risk would be expended for the least likely reward.

It would be pertinent to prioritize the search criteria based on the most likely sources of goods, such as the cafeteria storeroom, teachers' lounge and athletic event concession stands. At most, these areas would require three breaches since there would be three doors.

Our plan should include the identification of alternative exits and a good triage area where loot can be gathered if more is found than can be carried.

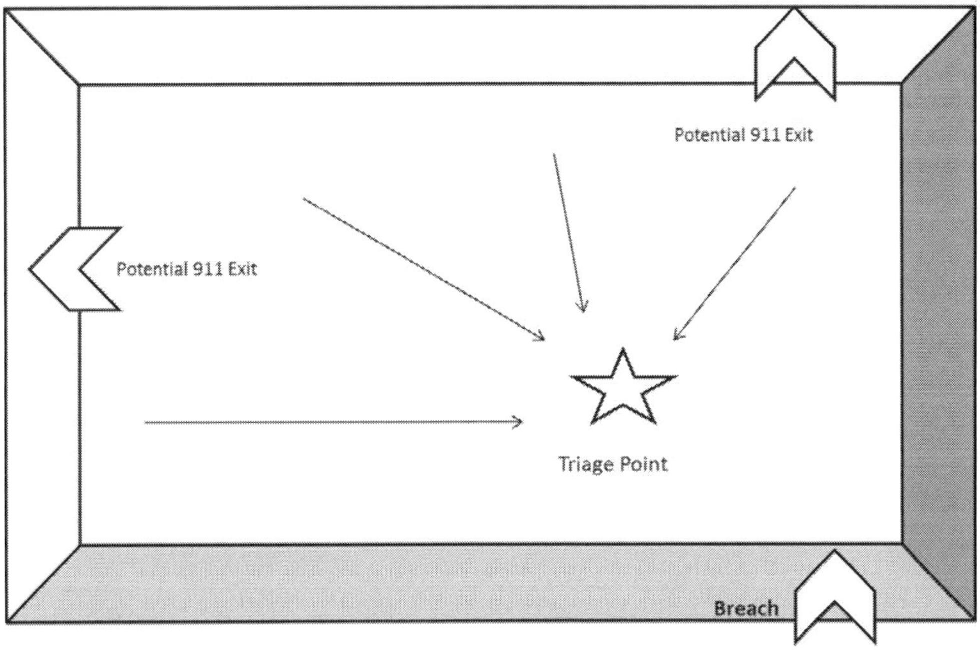

Operational Step	Notes
16:00 - Departure	5 hours before dark
16:30 - Cross CRoad/Stream	Unknown depth possible issue
17:30 - Cross 2nd Stream	Unknown depth possible issue
18:30 - Cross HW6	May require extra time for good crossing cover
19:30 Cross RR	May require extra time for good crossing cover
20:00 - Eat MRE	Make sure and store packaging
20:30 -Find/Construct Hide	Hide spot critical – must be able to construct in short time before dusk
21:30 -Set Trip wires	Silent trip wires for warning only – no noise makers
21:30 - Sleep	May sleep on ground if hide does not permit stringing of hammock
06:00 – Breakdown Camp	
06:30 - Defecate	
06:30 – 11:00 Build Raft	Observe and not area if task takes less time
11:05 - Meal	
12:00 – Rest/Sleep/Observe	
14:30 - Meal	Leave no trash
15:30 – Cross Stream	Leave at dusk
16:00 – Scout possible Breach	
16:30 – Breach	
17:00 – Verify Building empty	
18:00 – Set up Triage Point	
18:30 – Set up Security if necessary	Trip wires or noise makers. Make sure someone does not enter building without warning
19:00 – Keep watch/rest	Long Night ahead
06:00 – Snack	
06:30 – Use the facilities	Smoking in the boys room
07:00 – Begin search	
15:30 – Scout Exit	
16:00 – Exit with loot	Could require more than one trip
(etc...)	

11. OPERATING IN TEAMS

Any operation or mission will be more effective using teams comprised of multiple members. It's only common sense to divide the tasks and have redundancy available to reach a specific goal.

Operating in teams adds two requirements to all of the subject matter in this book:

- Command and Control

- Communications

A third "nice to have" capability would be cross training of specific skills.

Years ago, I used to enjoy paintball as a recreational activity. While it is simply a sport and not actual combat, one can garner certain lessons from the experience. One of the prime bits of wisdom I learned is that inexperienced people will naturally execute basic infantry tactics with little or no coaching. It is amazing to watch. What they don't bring to the table is the terminology.

11.1 COMMAND AND CONTROL

Someone has to be the leader, even if the group consists of only two people. Leadership is a broad and in-depth topic that is worthy of its own series of books (which already exist).

Leadership does not necessarily mean the traditional top-down organizational structure that is used in most military units. Special Forces teams often have "skull sessions" where everyone, regardless of rank, participates in the planning of an operation or mission. Modern day, conventional military forces have learned from the success of their special comrades and have more relaxed planning sessions among the officers and senior enlisted men.

While allowing participation in the planning is wise leadership, ultimately someone has to resolve disputes and make the final decision. Someone has to be responsible.

If the group is large enough, a structure may be required. Except in special circumstances, it is difficult for one individual to directly control more than 12 individuals in a stressful situation.

It is an interesting topic of how leadership is established out of a random group of individuals. Some historical societies value wisdom and respect experience, while others choose the strongest as the leader.

If you are going to be part of a group of preppers who intend to operate together, the command and control structure should be implemented before the SHTF or trouble could linger on the horizon.

11.2 COMMUNICATIONS

Communications, for us preppers, can be broken down into three separate parts:

-Terminology

-Tactical Communications

-Strategic Communications

These are fancy, military sounding terms that really are very simple to understand and implement.

11.2.1 TERMINOLOGY

There are dozens of terms used to describe infantry maneuvers and actions. Different terms, used to describe the exact same action, exist even today across units and branches of the military. While certain basics are universal, such as the term flanking, other phrases, such a "buddy rushing" would result in a questioning look if used in certain combat units. Army units tend to use the phrase "bounding" to describe the same exact maneuver, while I have only heard Marines use "buddy rushing." The determination of your team's vocabulary really depends on the roster and experience of the members.

The actual terms are really unimportant. What is critical is everyone is on the same page of the dictionary. One way to speak the same language is to get a book on small unit maneuvers and have it become the standard.

The most comprehensive field manual I have found on this topic is the *U.S. Department of the Army FM 7-8.* It is available from numerous sources, and while it contains far more information than most preppers will ever use, the sections on Movement Techniques (2-10) and Actions at Danger Areas (2-11) and others regarding movement and communications are worthy of study.

There are other good sources of small unit tactical actions that can obtained as well. Some are more detailed than others, and which one should become your group's standard reference depends on you. You can even make up your own. If your family is a fan of American football, then you will find commonality using terms from that sport. What is important is that everyone understands the meaning of each phrase or term.

EXERCISE

Pick three or four basic tactical actions and see if you and your group can execute. Some examples would be:

-Bounding

-Enveloping

-Advance to contact

-Safety Egress

You can do this in your backyard (on a small scale) or at a park. There are several games you can make out of this if your group involves teenagers or young adults. Rather than "flag football" you can play "take the flag" or other creations.

Drawing overhead views (sandboxing) tools can be helpful in communicating to the team. Just pretend you are a basketball coach diagraming a play.

11.2.2 TACTICAL COMMUNICATIONS

Once everyone understands the terminology, the next capability you need to establish for a group is communications. Relaying instructions, situational awareness, status, and other information while in the field has always been a problem with military forces.

Preppers need to establish two basic communications capabilities. The first is silent signals. Hand signals, written instructions, and other methods of noiseless knowledge transfer can be important. Most military units know and understand 20 or less hand signals, and there are numerous sources on the internet available identifying what they are. Just like our terminology, a standard for your group should be established. If this is too difficult, passing notes can be effective in some situations.

The second is long-range communications. Practically every sporting goods store carries inexpensive radios with ranges up to five miles. Many of these are rechargeable, waterproof devices designed for hunting or other outdoor activities. If you have prepared some method of recharging batteries, these are an excellent option. A small solar charger can keep these critical devices in operating order.

One word of advice on selecting radios – make sure they can operate with ear buds or other push-to-talk headphones. As depicted in numerous movies, a radio squawking at the wrong time can give away your position and lead to problems.

EXERCISE

Purchase a set of radios and go to a park or remote area with your group. Pick a leader, someone to run the exercise. Agree upon a rally point (parking lot?) and then spread out.

Using the radios, guide everyone back to the rally point, *in a specific order*. This simple exercise will help with radio communications and protocol. More advanced games and exercises can be devised over time. Use the equipment, and become confident with it.

11.2.3 STRATEGIC COMMUNICATIONS

To perform the tactical actions outlined in this book, you have to plan. When operating in a group, everyone has to know and understand the plan. Even when operating alone, the steps, timetables, and equipment lists should be written out. This becomes even more important when you have a team.

There are all kinds of waterproof paper and writing utensils available. These are inexpensive pieces of kit, yet they are often overlooked by the typical prepper. Have some method of writing things down. This is used for not only communication of the plan, but also when scouting or performing reconnaissance. Sometimes referred to as "all weather paper," this gear should be stocked in quantity for TEOTWAWKI.

There are also some procedures that can be established as a preparation. These items might be more policy than actual communications and often involve determining your ethical boundaries. These would involve such topics as whether your group honors a white flag. What is your protocol for strangers who wander into your BOL? Can anyone initiate shooting?

The modern military has hundreds (perhaps thousands) of manuals and guidelines. While their needs far outstrip anything the typical prepper group would require, it makes sense to have as much written down and agreed upon ahead of time. If an event occurs, the stress levels and indecision will be difficult enough. Why not use modern word processors, laser printers, and office supply stores while they still exist?

12. IN SUMMARY

I don't know of a single prepper who has any desire to utilize the content of this book. Most hope their preparations will carry them through even the darkest of times. We want to hunt, trap, fish and raise gardens for our survival, not take what doesn't originally belong to us.

Within our means, most of us prepare to a level that we believe will allow for a reasonable quality of life should the SHTF. Most of us worry that we have overlooked something that may become critical when the stores are no longer open, and there is no rule of law.

My grandparents lived through the Great Depression. They were frugal people who, even after achieving modest wealth, worked hard on hot summer afternoons tending a garden. My grandmother canned everything from cream corn to green beans. One of my favorite times was when the potatoes were ready to be dug. I would rub the dirt off, slice them open with my pocketknife and eat them raw. Maybe it's just the "good old days" syndrome, but nothing seemed to taste like freshly picked produce from that garden.

I learned a lot from my grandparents. They both remained mentally sharp into their later years, and we would spend countless hours talking about everything from the Great Depression to WWII. Some of their stories seemed unbelievable at the time. The concept of ration coupons during WWII was completely foreign to a child raised in the 1960s. Everyone avoided driving, even when gasoline was available, because you couldn't buy a tire anywhere.

One of the most important lessons they tried to pass on to me was "never take anything for granted." My great grandfather, a man in his prime during the depression, struggled to read because his eyes were naturally degrading. Eyeglasses were not available. As I get older, I worry about a post-collapse world and my eyesight. *Will I be able to see given I have to get new glasses every few years now?*

One of the most insightful of his tales involved shoes. The local church had a "shoe exchange" bulletin board during the depression. If you have children, you know they outgrow shoes a few times a year during spurts. While I went barefoot as much as possible during the summer, in colder months this was not possible. *What are people going to do for shoes and clothing if they have little ones in a SHTF world?*

During the depression, some species of deer were hunted to the brink of extinction. I remember my great uncles telling stories of deer being common in the area, yet when I was a child, they were rare. *What if survival plans involve hunting the local deer population for food, and the same thing happened?* Now, 35 years later, they have made a comeback to that area. The same can be said of wild turkeys.

Many of us believe we will grow our own food. Our preparations have enough store bought calories to make it through until the next harvest season. I was going over my plan with a new prepper friend not long ago. He pondered all of my resources and simple plan. "But what if a drought hits? What about insects or an early frost?"

We discussed the fact that it is virtually impossible to prepare for any and all eventualities. It is certainly possible that no matter how prepared we may be, lawlessness may continue for an undetermined amount of time. It is also probable that those who did not plan for a post-apocalyptic situation will take drastic measures to survive---measures that might include breaching our BOL and taking our supplies. I informed him that if a wave of events hit, I would have to resort to scavenging and looting to survive. That I was prepared to do what it takes to survive and felt confident in my skills.

He said, "I wouldn't have any idea how to start preparing for something like that."

A copy of this book is on its way to him.

Appendix A – Load Bearing Equipment

As you have read the above work, it has been repeated numerous times the value of a good load carry system. The book ***The TEOTWAWKI Tuxedo*** contains a complete reference on the subject. The following information contains excerpts from that work.

The two most popular types of military load-bearing equipment are MOLLE and ALICE:

MOLLE (*pronounced Molly*) is an acronym for:

MOdular
Lightweight
Load carrying
Equipment

MOLLE replaced ALICE:
All-purpose
Lightweight
Individual
Carry
Equipment

Components for both types of systems are readily available at numerous retail outlets, with Army Surplus stores being very cost effective. Since MOLLE is the newer of the two systems, it will be used in all examples.

A quick primer follows:

The MOLLE system allows the connection of dozens of different types of pouches, bags, flashlights, tools and containers.

MOLLE equipment has two basic parts, the **Base** and **Attachments**.

The Base item, whether it is a vest, belt, pack or other component, will be manufactured with rows of what appear to be loops sewn horizontally to the item every inch.

MOLLE Base shown with a marker in the loops.

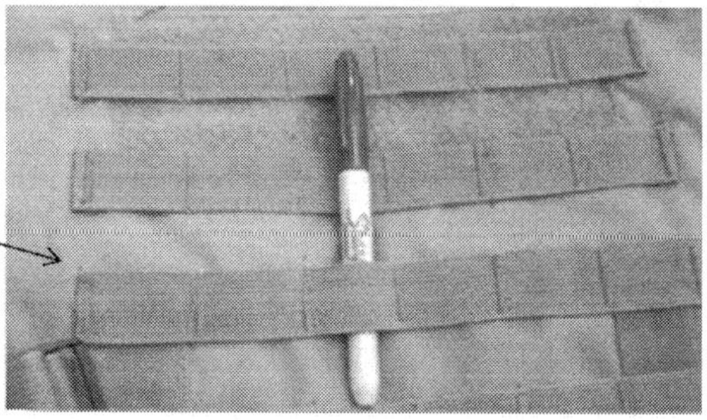

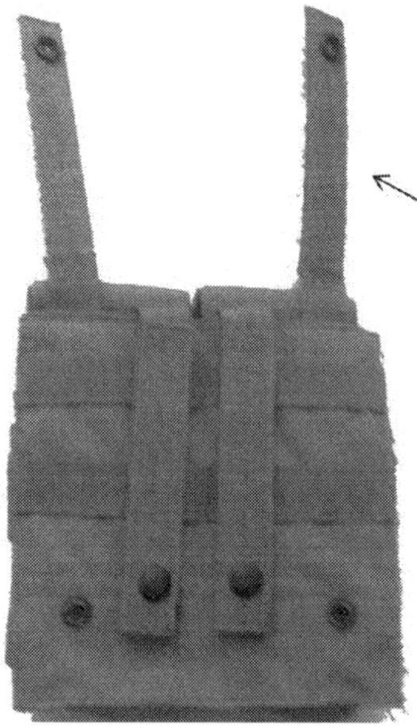

MOLLE pouch with two of four straps extended.

The Straps are "woven" through the loops on the base and then secured via the snaps.

The Attachment, whether it is a pouch, holster, container, canteen or other item has a series of vertical straps and snaps.

MOLLE Attachments come in hundreds of different configurations from different manufacturers.

The Base

For the average survivalist, there are four relevant types of **Base** Carriers that everyone should become familiar with:

(1) Plate Carriers

(2) Load Vests

(3) Chest Rigs

(4) Belts

Each type of Base unit has strengths and weaknesses. As the methodology in Chapter 2 suggests, any equipment purchase is more valuable when the item has dual purpose. Hunting, fishing, camping and even weapons training classes are some alternative uses for MOLLE.

Plate Carriers look like a vest and are designed to carry body armor plates, or Kevlar plates, to stop bullets and fragments. While body armor is becoming more common and affordable, most preppers will probably choose soft-sided armor over actual plate armor.

Load Vests are almost identical to Plate Carriers except they don't have the internal pouches. Vests provide the most real estate for attachments. They also tend to have the widest area of support over the shoulders, so the straps don't dig in as much.

Chest Rigs differ from Vests in that they have straps or suspenders over your shoulders to carry the load. Chest Rigs are normally smaller than vests and open in the back – thus they are cooler to wear. They don't have as much real estate for Attachments and often do not have a snug fit like vests. The equipment may shift around more with a rig, but they are adjustable.

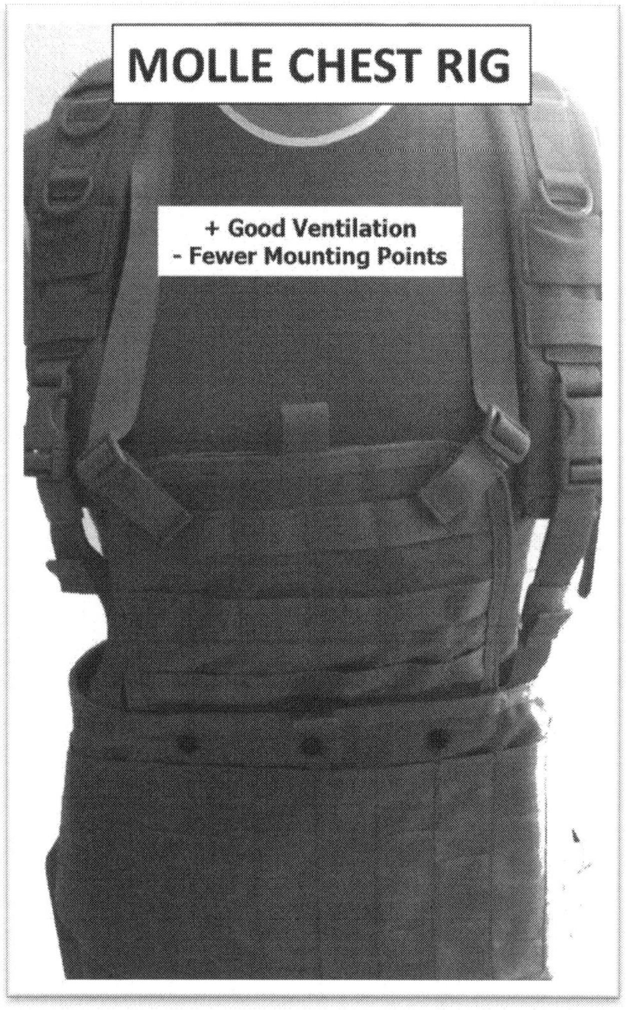

Belts are sometimes called war belts or battle belts and are basically the same concept as a policeman's duty belt – except for MOLLE. Belts typically have the least amount of real estate of any type of MOLLE Base. Some of the larger Chest Rigs are actually a belt, but also have suspenders to help support the weight.

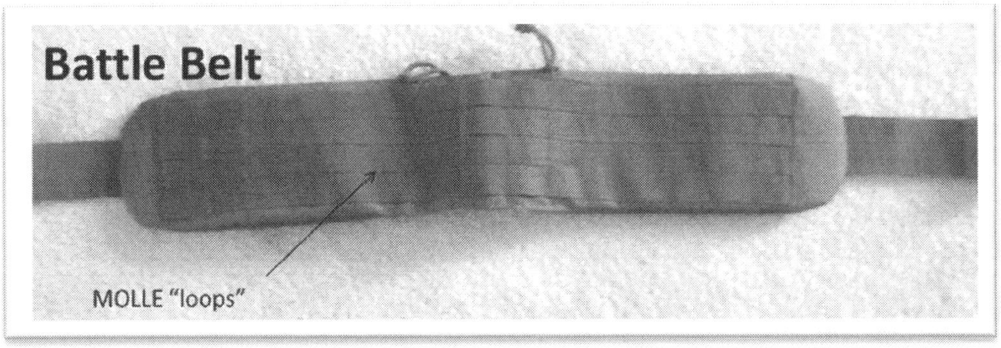

Attachments

Attachments come in so many different shapes, sizes, colors and configurations some manufacturers have entire catalogs devoted to them. What is important is that they ALL will fit on the Base unit. The connection is standard, just like a hitch on a railway car.

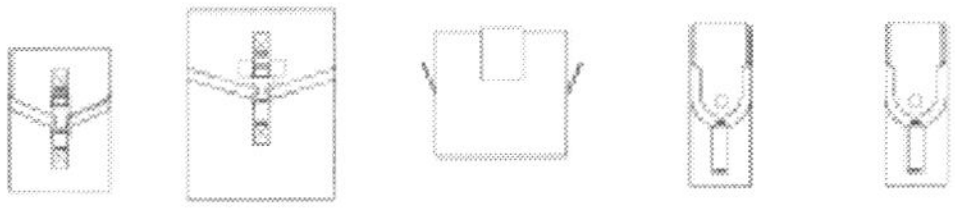

Most army surplus stores or "Duty" clothing outlets carry dozens of different types of MOLLE Attachments for just about every possible configuration. Here are a few of the more common ones:

-> **Medical kit**

-> **Dump pouch** – used to store empty magazines or other discarded items you don't want to leave on the ground. (Empty magazines and power bar wrappers)

-> **Holsters** for your secondary (pistol)

-> **Flare** pouches

-> **Grenade** pouches (smoke grenades for most of us)

-> **Weapons** maintenance kit and spares

-> **Night vision**

-> **Radio** or Walkie-Talkie

Some MOLLE Attachments are quite large. The picture below shows a common MOLLE dump pouch with a standard tissue box inside and plenty of room left over.

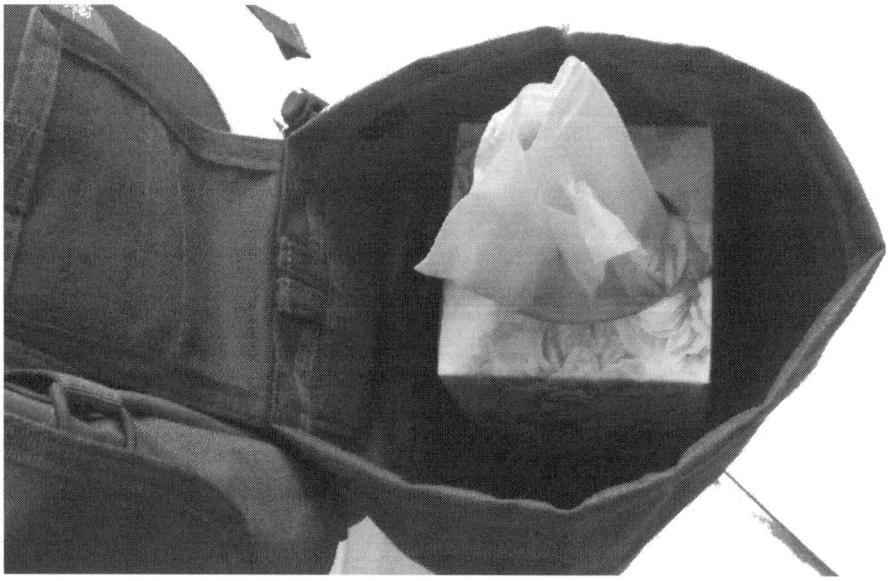

17837645R00101

Made in the USA
Lexington, KY
03 October 2012